DONKEYS' YEARS ON THE MALVERN HILLS

230 illustrations, 70 in colour.

Original map showing paths and bridleways made by benefactors since about 1800 and used as the main hire-donkey routes. Norman May's Guide to Malvern, 1886.

O— Approximate position of some other sites noted in this book, 2008.

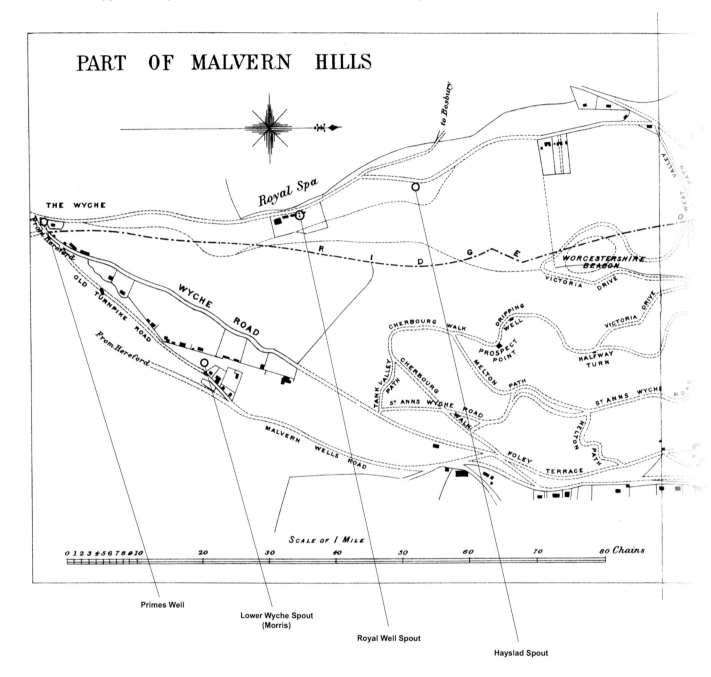

Primes Well

Lower Wyche Spout
(Morris)

Royal Well Spout

Hayslad Spout

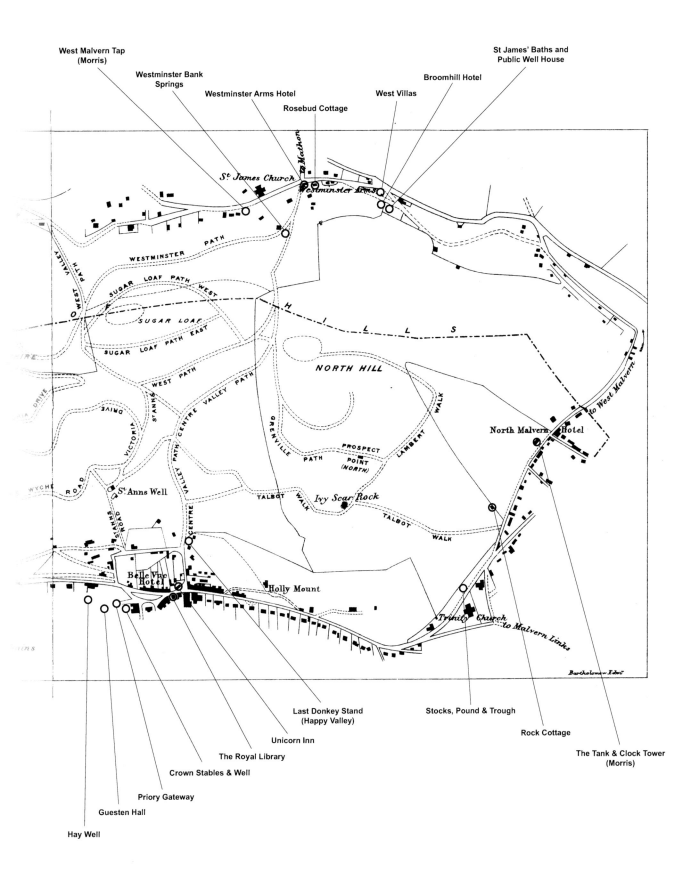

West Malvern Tap
(Morris)

Westminster Bank
Springs

Westminster Arms Hotel

Rosebud Cottage

St James' Baths and
Public Well House

Broomhill Hotel

West Villas

St James Church

Westminster Arms

to Mathon

WESTMINSTER PATH

WEST VALLEY PATH

SUGAR LOAF PATH

WEST PATH

SUGAR LOAF

SUGAR LOAF PATH EAST

H I L L S

NORTH HILL

LAMBERT WALK

DRIVE

VICTORIA DRIVE

ST ANNS DRIVE

CENTRE VALLEY PATH

GRENVILLE PATH

PROSPECT
POINT
(NORTH)

to West Malvern

North Malvern Hotel

St Anns Well

WYCHE ROAD

ST ANNS ROAD

CENTRE

TALBOT WALK

Ivy Scar Rock

TALBOT WALK

Belle Vue
Hotel

Holly Mount

Trinity Church

to Malvern Links

Bartholomew Edin

Last Donkey Stand
(Happy Valley)

Stocks, Pound & Trough

Rock Cottage

Unicorn Inn

The Royal Library

The Tank & Clock Tower
(Morris)

Crown Stables & Well

Priory Gateway

Guesten Hall

Hay Well

DONKEYS' YEARS ON
THE MALVERN HILLS

A History of the Famous Hill Donkeys
at Malvern's Springs, Spouts and Holy Wells

by Rose Garrard

Dedicated to the memory of my brother
Dr Timothy Garrard
Barrister, Archaeologist and Historian
1943 - 2007

Garrard Art Publications

Garrard Art Publications

ISBN: 978-1-905795-18-5

Digital Production by Aspect Design
Printed by Aspect Design
89 Newtown Road, Malvern, Worcs. WR14 1AN
United Kingdom
Tel: 01684 561567
E-mail: books@aspect-design.net
www.aspect-design.net

Garrard Art Publications; Malvern; England

DONKEYS' YEARS ON THE MALVERN HILLS

A History of the Famous Hill Donkeys at Malvern's Springs, Spouts and Holy Wells

LIST OF CONTENTS

Donkey and driver waiting for hire on Victoria Drive, Foley Terrace, Great Malvern, 1909.

DONKEYS' YEARS ON THE MALVERN HILLS

A History of the Famous Hill Donkeys
at Malvern's Springs, Spouts and Holy Wells

Prelude

Two thousand years ago donkeys were regarded as high status animals essential for transport and travel. In the less distant past they came to be viewed as dumb, comical and stubborn beasts and today, at best, they are merely regarded as 'cute' rides for children on English seaside holidays.

Perhaps because of their devaluation in our eyes, the history of the once famous Malvern Hills' donkeys has almost faded away, but in this little book I hope to begin to redress the balance.

For many years I have collected objects, books and images from Malvern's past, which included some pictures and incidental comments on the hills' donkeys. Now with further research, plus texts, reminiscences and other images generously contributed by friends, local residents, collectors and institutions, the important role of donkeys here from medieval times through to 'modern' Malvern has begun to be revealed, alongside the development of the springs, spouts and holy wells. This donkey history also gives a glimpse of the social and economic divisions

Donkey ride at Barry Island c1920.

between the gentry and the poor, particularly during the apparently glamourous years of the 'water cure' when Malvern was also very famous for its hill donkeys.

ACKNOWLEDGEMENTS

My sincerest thanks for all the support given on this venture by those who have generously contributed help, information, images, texts and personal recollections, including Allan Knight, Paul Clifton, Ken Davis, Lord Sandys, David & Dinah Prentice, Peter Smith, Christine & Roland Bannister, Tim & Anna Brazier, Michael & Sylvia Gardener, Jim Black, Jonathan Penley, Marjorie King, Anna & Colin Jackson, Carole Wheeler, William Herring, Ken Rickards, Heather Gilderdale, John Redman, Glen Harnden, John Griffith, Julia Thomas, Tanya Ganlen, Dudley Brook, Brian Iles, Paula & George Waugh, Marie Myers & Andrew Cooksy, Ray Roberts, the Malvern Museum, Malvern Hills Conservators, Malvern Library, the Donkey Sanctuary and Cardiff University. The author also acknowledges with grateful thanks the many written records listed in the bibliography on page 155 that have helped to make this book possible. Every attempt has been made to trace and obtain copyright permissions on all images included here.

1 - Brief World History of the Donkey

Today it is estimated that there are about 44 million donkeys in the world, although it's thought that the real number is much higher. The vast majority of donkeys are used for the same types of work that they have been doing for the last 6000 years. Their most common role in the East is for transport, whether for riding, as pack animals, or for pulling carts, and in farming for ploughing and as dairy animals for their milk, while in the richer Western world the majority are now kept as pets. Donkeys often live for twenty-five years or more although a forty-year-old donkey is considered to be elderly. Some have been recorded as living to the ripe old age of sixty, their longevity giving rise to the saying *"for donkeys' years"*.

Because all the original equine species living here in the western hemisphere became extinct at the end of the last Ice Age, the ancient ancestors of today's donkeys were bred from the surviving wild asses of Africa and Asia. The larger ass and smaller donkey were first domesticated around 4000 BC at approximately the same time as the horse, and have since spread around the world. By 1800 BC the ass had reached the Middle East where the trading city of Damascus was referred to as the *"City of Asses"* in cuneiform texts. At a time when horses were reserved solely for warfare, powerful kings such as Solomon were the only ones who could afford to import asses and donkeys from Egypt and so they became a revered status symbol.

Inside a funerary complex at Abydos in Egypt, archaeologists have recently uncovered the skeletons of ten donkeys dating from 3000 B.C., buried on their own with full

Donkey with panniers collecting the grain harvest, from painted mural in the tomb of Hor-Aha, 1250 BC Ancient Egypt. Drawing by Rose Garrard. Previous page - *Balaam, Nurenberg Chronicles, 1493.*

honours and without any human or other animal remains. The only animals buried in the tombs of the kings themselves have symbolic or religious significance. No other animals have ever been found at such sites. *"It's not exactly what an Egyptologist would expect to find. They were very surprised to find no human remains and no funerary goods and instead to find ten donkeys. It was a spectacular discovery."* said Dr. Marshall, a professor of archaeology at Washington University, one of the few researchers in the world dedicated to understanding the history of donkeys.

The domesticated donkey became an important pack animal for people living in the Egyptian and Nubian regions as it could easily carry a quarter of its own body weight. The historian Michelet devoted a whole chapter to the donkey. *"This amiable animal, pride of the East, which every*

Donkey with panniers carrying a child, Egypt 1940s.

year like a royal magus entered Babylon in triumph with its joyous harvest, was feasted and honoured. He was given the respectful name of Bel-Peor, Lord Donkey. He was treated with even greater respect in Syria, where according to the prophet his coarse gaiety and amorous gifts, his superiority over men, made him the wonder of the Syrians.

… In fact he is a demon, Bel-Phegor, the demon both impure and kind, who is of use to everybody for everything, and lets himself be bridled and ridden … and without pity he was charged with back-breaking burdens. In the desert there was a celebration for the Feast of the Donkey. He stepped out boldly to the North and to the West, preaching the culture of the vine, to give wine."

The Old Testament book of Genesis records that the donkey was held in high enough esteem for its name to be used for royalty, where the King of Sechem, now Nablus, has the first name of *"Hamor"* the word for donkey. Another biblical story tells of a donkey becoming a prophet, when King Balek summons Balaam the soothsayer to him to lay a curse on the Israelites. Balaam sets off to the King, but when climbing a mountain his donkey halts because it sees the angel of God ahead.

12th century carved capitol of a pillar showing Balaam on his donkey, from the Church of St Andoche, France.

Wood carving of Mary and baby Jesus on a donkey, Italian 15th century.

In the miracle of St Anthony a starving donkey chose to kneel before the Eucharist held up by the Saint, rather than eat from its pagan master's hand.

Despite being beaten three times the donkey refuses to go any further. Only then does the angel become visible to Balaam and instead of fullfilling the King's malevolent instructions, the donkey tells Balaam to obey God's command and bless the Israelites on the plain below forever. To this day the mountain where the animal spoke is called 'the Donkey'.

Originally the larger ass and smaller donkey were among the domesticated animals that used to carry silk to the Mediterranean along the 'Silk Road' from China. The journey along this overland trade route was over 6,000 km and took several years to complete through the Middle East to Greece and Italy and as matings happened en-route the mixing of previously unique breeds from Africa and Asia occurred. Syria produced at least three breeds of donkeys, including a saddle breed with an easy gait often favoured by women.

Old Testament and Hebrew Bible texts often specify whether a person rode a donkey, as this was seen as an indicator of a person's wealth and high status at a time when travelling on foot was just for commoners. In early Christian symbolism the donkey not only stood for affluence, but also for humility, patience and courage. Traditionally Mary, the mother of Jesus, was portrayed as riding safely on a donkey with her baby, who was of course born in a manger with an ox and an ass standing by, and the Bible describes the triumphal entry of Jesus into Jerusalem riding on a donkey. However, in later times when the aristocracy rode mainly on horses, depicting the messiah as riding on a donkey came to have a different connotation. It now indicated a simple, sober way of life, avoiding luxury, evident in the descriptions of saints such as Francis of Assisi riding donkeys. The donkey was also regarded as an animal which could be trusted to warn of danger and was sometimes even believed to instinctively sense right from wrong.

Donkeys are still popular in the Middle East today for farming, as dairy animals and as guides. *"For *mapping and tracing the routes he is a master, a pioneer; he goes ahead and one can trace behind him the future path and its every short cut. He is the guide of the flocks and of the caravans, taking charge and in the lead. There is in Lebanon a whole region named after his kind, the region called 'The Ass', al-Debeh, the very area where the alphabet was invented. … Once upon a time every home in Lebanon had its donkey and one met him everywhere, in the alleys and in the fields. He knew perfectly all the ways, storing*

Learning to plough with donkeys in Kenya. Dr E. Svendsen, 1993. Courtesy of the Donkey Sanctuary, Devon

them in his memory like a computer, returning by himself to his stable and his manger and just signalling his presence so someone would come and take his load off his back. He was there ready for work in the fields, for ploughing for helping with the grape harvest, bringing in the crops, carrying from the mill and from the fountain – and well smartened up he was a mount for any journey. Firm and undaunted, he kept perfect balance and never slipped." (Lebanese Art by Joseph Matar, translated by K.J. Mortimer, 2007)

A donkey walking a wheel to draw up drinking water from the Great Well at Carisbrooke Castle, Isle of Wight, c1910.

As the cultivation of the grape spread in Greece, the donkey was found to be ideal animal for working the narrow paths between the vines and so became most associated with Dionysus the god of wine. The Romans also valued the donkey and every year on the 8th June a festival was celebrated in Rome during which the Vestal Virgins covered a donkey with flowers. The donkey was also sometimes used as a sacrificial animal in their religious rituals, as well as for transport and agriculture. The Greeks and Romans spread the use of donkeys for cultivating vineyards throughout the Mediterranean countries to Spain, where they are still common.

The Spanish Conqistadors took horses and donkeys to the South Americas and Christopher Columbus brought four jacks (male donkeys) and two jennys (female donkeys) to the New World in 1495. The donkey only became widespread in North America in the mid 1800s when it was found useful as a pack animal by miners and gold prospectors. They preferred this animal to ponies, due to its ability to carry heavy tools, supplies and ore safely in rough terrain, as well as for its sociability and companionship. This often meant the donkeys would simply follow behind their owner without being led on reigns, allowing the miner a free hand, often to carry a rifle. As mining increased in scale to become an industrial operation, the miners' donkeys became redundant and were simply turned loose into the American deserts where their descendants can still be found roaming wild.

Detail of a medieval manuscript showing a naked wild-man driving a donkey ridden by a monkey.

Having been the companion of man for thousands of years, the donkey also often appears as a character in literature from Homer to Shakespeare, from ancient mythology, to fairy stories and fables. In Chaucer's Canterbury Tales one medieval pilgrim, the Wife of Bath, tells how King Midas had his ears changed to those of a donkey by Appollo, as a punishment for judging against him in favor of Pan in a musical contest. The King sought to hide his donkey's ears in his hair and by wearing a cap, but his secret still got out as it was whispered continually on the wind. For many in the west the donkey became an object of ridicule because of its large ears and is now often a symbol of stupidity, laziness and obstinacy. But in the Middle East today, ownership of many donkeys is still seen as a sign of God's blessing by people of most religions and the donkey is regarded as a creature of courage, devotion, gentleness and humility.

Donkey gargoyle, high up on the 13th century Church of St Mary the Virgin, the first official building of Oxford University. Photo courtesy of Marie Myers and Andrew Cooksy, San Diego State University.

The Donkey

G.K. Chesterton

When fishes flew and forests walked
And figs grew upon thorn,
Some moment when the moon was blood
Then surely I was born;

With monstrous head and sickening cry
And ears like errant wings,
The devil's walking parody
On all four-footed things.

The tattered outlaw of the earth,
Of ancient crooked will;
Starve, scourge, deride me: I am dumb,
I keep my secret still.

Fools! For I also had my hour;
One far fierce hour and sweet:
There was a shout about my ears,
And palms before my feet.

Now we are looking at each other.

Donkeys were first brought to Britain in the Roman invasion of 43 A.D. with the soldiers of Emperor Claudius, mainly as pack animals carrying supplies and trade goods. The Roman Army used donkeys as beasts of burden, whereas horses were usually reserved for soldiers and warfare. The Legions were responsible for the movement of domesticated donkeys into Northern Europe, where they were then used to cultivate the Romans' new vineyards as far north as France and Germany.

One of three tracks through the Malvern Hills used to be called the Wyche Pass and was on an ancient trade route; the word wyche coming later from the Saxon word 'wich' for a street or track often associated with salt. As the track was on the 'Upper Saltway', one of the Roman salt trade routes from the Droit-'wich' brine springs to their frontiers in South Wales, sure-footed donkeys and mules were probably first used in the Malverns to

Donkey carriage at "The Wytch Pass", by Newman 1869.

The early Wyche Cutting, c1850.

carry the salt in panniers up this once narrow hill track. This rocky path originally ran up behind the present buildings on the north-eastern side of the hills, then down along the Purlieu in the west. The years of work on cutting through the granite hill to widen and lower this pass into a road was not begun until 1836 and after this it became known as Wyche Cutting. There is some evidence that the Romans travelled through the hill passes from Droitwich, their most important local settlement when Worcester was only a small village specialising in iron smelting. There have been some Roman pottery finds in the north Malverns and also near Madresfield, and in 1847 two pottery urns were uncovered at the Wynds Point quarry, in the pass beside the Herefordshire Beacon, containing *"a large find of Roman coins dating between A.D. 286 and 311, some of them apparently in mint-state."* (*Worcestershire in English History, Alec Macdonald 1943*)

A map of 1633 shows a spring at Wyche Cutting named as Primes Spring, earlier in about 1400 it was referred to as Primes Well. The actual site of this well is now thought to be under the grassy bank beside the gate to High Land Cottage. In the Roman period the top of this rugged pass would have been an ideal watering place for pack animals on their long journey. Some say that the nearby Pyxie Path at Wyche Cutting was named after the sign for Christ, the pyx, emblazoned on the breastplates of the soldiers of the first Christian Emperor, Constantine. It is also likely that the first missionaries rode up through the pass on donkeys or 'Jerusalem ponies' as they had become the favoured steeds of the early Christians when spreading the Gospel. Later, medieval monks and pilgrims travelling to visit the Cathedral tombs of St Wulstan and St Oswald in Worcester or St Thomas in Hereford followed this route via St Thomas' Well, now inside a cottage near the Royal Well at Wyche Cutting.

In Britain from about 250 B.C. the Celtic Dobunni people revered the waters of the springs and wells of the Malvern Hills and regarded these sources as sacred. When the first Christian missionaries arrived in the Malverns from Europe, they used these springs to baptise the local pagan population and so the waters became known as 'holy', hence Holy Well in Malvern Wells. But a number of other sources were also considered as holy wells at that time, including Moorall's Well, now lost, and Walm's Well below British Camp, long famous for curing skin diseases, both of which were said to have been named after the earliest missionaries here from Europe. In the 11th century the 'wilderness' of the 'Malvern Forest' was sparsely inhabited by solitary hermits who lived beside these water sources, then by Benedictine monks who established the Priory at Great Malvern in 1085 and Little Malvern Priory in 1127, relying on the springs for their domestic supplies and probably using donkeys for transport and agriculture.

"From the most remote times, the maimed, the lame, the halt, the blind, the leper sought to lave in the health giving waters, and to be made whole." (May's Guide to Malvern, 1886) It's also likely that in accordance with their vow of poverty, these Benedictine monks would have used the humble donkey to transport the frailest of the sick to the holy wells on the slippery hill slopes. At Little Malvern the 12th century monks used the waters at Holy Well for healing the sick by wrapping them in wet cloths, a method that was still in use in Malvern in the 1890s. There was also another ancient holy well much closer to the monastery that supplied the monks, the local villagers and diseased visitors. Said to have been the original holy well, it was known as 'Mary's Well' or 'Ditchford Spring' and was still being visited for its curative waters in the 1850s. Sadly a large electricity pylon now occupies the site beside the Ledbury Road but a spring, piped underground to the brook below, still exists in the centre of the field.

There is also still a spring flow into a tank above the cottage gardens, which in turn feeds a cattle trough nearby and may continue into the old fishponds beside the church.

"There is a spring called Ditchford's Well, which rises in an ash coppice, about five hundred yards from Little Malvern Church, on the Ledbury Road. This spring, we are informed, is the original one and that it was noticed long before Holy Well." (Chambers' General History of Malvern, 1817)

Little Malvern Church and old pond, 1874.

Early 19th century drawing of the Priory by "John Doe", with donkey rider on the path that became Church Street.

At Great Malvern Priory during the 11th century, water from the nearby 'Hay Well' was piped to the monastery, while the even older 'St Agnes Well' supplied their adjacent farm. The presence of a 'Leper's Tile' in the church, dated 1456, reminds us that very sickly patients were also coming to both the Hay Well and St Ann's Well on the Worcestershire Beacon, to benefit from their apparent healing properties. The Latin text on the four-tile pattern translates as *"Have pity on me, have pity on me, O ye my friends, for the hand of God has touched me"*. At the Priory it's believed that lepers were hidden from view inside the northwest entrance to the church, in a wooden shelter below the first north window, which consequently has a higher sill to prevent other worshippers seeing them. *"In the middle ages there were many people smitten with such diseases as required isolation from their fellows and separate places were provided for them in the churches."* (*Malvern Priory Church, Stevens, 1913*)

22

Donkeys would have been the most practical way of transporting the leprous, lame and infirm up to the higher holy wells. The first mention of *"St Anne's Well"* on the Worcestershire Beacon was by the Bishop of Westminster in 1282 and appears in the parish records. The origins of both the well and the name Anne or Ann are thought to be much earlier, deriving from the Celtic word *"Tan"* for beacon or fire. Pilgrims had

been visiting this holy well for centuries and it has sometimes been associated with Werstan the hermit whose legend was illustrated in the Priory windows in 1465. His little hermitage and oratory, *"St Myghelles"* chapel, was built about four hundred years before, on a ledge near Rose Bank some distance below the very steep slope to the well.

An apparently surreal 15th century image of a donkey can still be seen in the east window of the Great Malvern Priory. This once magnificent stained glass window illustrates the Life of Christ, one panel showing his 'Entry into Jerusalem' riding on a bright blue donkey. Blue is a highly significant colour in Catholicism symbolising heaven and faithfulness and in line with medieval rules of monastic art is usually reserved for the Virgin Mary's robe as 'Queen of Heaven'. But

East window of Great Malvern Priory showing "Christ's Entry Into Jerusalem" riding on a blue donkey. Drawing by Rose Garrard, 2008.

this Malvern donkey was endowed with the colour blue and consequently with its spiritual qualities, suggesting that at the Priory the donkey was held in high esteem. Even today blue vestments are not authorized for use in the Catholic Church, except in some isolated areas that had special permission to use the colour, such as the Order of the Knights of the Garter created originally in the 14th century by Edward III, who still wear 'heavenly' blue velvet robes.

As was usual in medieval Europe, the monks may have also used donkeys to cultivate their farmland on the lower Great Malvern hillside, perhaps carrying the harvest back in panniers to the Priory Farmhouse, originally on the site of the present Baptist Church in Abbey Road.   There were orchards in South Field, now the Abbey Road area, and the monks' terraced vineyards are believed to have been to the north of the Priory. *"Traces of ancient vineyards are abundant in this country. … Some writers have supposed that the Romans planted vines in Britain. Tacitus intimates that the olive and the vine were deficient here; but it is clear from Bede and others that they were cultivated at a subsequent period, and perhaps were neglected only when the inhabitants found they could purchase better wines at lower prices from France."* *(Notes and Queries for Worcestershire, John Noake 1856)*   The Priory vineyard area has recently become the car park for Waitrose but until 1999 it contained a large rectangular well known as the 'Vine Well'. This has now been demolished and the water diverted to a new, but polluted, outlet spout named 'Rose Gully' in Back Lane, off Graham Road.

Donkey being used to carry the grape harvest in panniers with liners, 19th century French tile.

The Vine Well, Great Malvern, 1997.

The Old Town

Ivan Theofilov, 1931

Your ancient floors float among the stars.
Blue donkeys graze the silence around.
The Roman road leads down along matrimonial
chandeliers.
A cry out of woman's flesh calls in the clock.
Violet-colored philistines go to bed in the deep
houses,
they hear the pig, the hens, the train, the mouse.
The darkness dawns with quick sensual pupils.
The bridal veil flies away with the chimney's breath.
Blue donkeys run on the moonlit roofs.
Saints take off in a cloud from whitewashed churches,
with blood-soaked lambs they welcome the bridal veil.

(Translated from Bulgarian by Zdravka Mihaylova)

3 - Donkey Power at the Holy Wells

From 1066 until 1632 the English monarchs reserved a large area of land called the 'Malvern Forest' for royal hunting, which was governed by their own severe 'forest law'. As well as supplying deer, wild boar and other animals for the royal table, the valuable products of the forest included wild honey and felled wood. This timber was traded for Droitwich salt and used for firing the brine pits where the salt was extracted by evaporation. These lands of the royal forest stretched from the river Severn at Upton bridge in the east, to the top of the Malvern Hills in the west and from the river Teme at Powick in the north, to *"Corse forest"* in the south, including both Great and Little Malvern. Hunting here without a royal warrant was forbidden and any inhabitants over twelve years of age had to swear an oath *"to be of good behaviour towards his Majesty's wild beasts"*. As the poor were not allowed to catch wild animals for food they could not survive easily in the district, but *"If a deer was found killed, an inquest as to the cause of death was held. The flesh was afterwards given to the nearest hospital, or to the poor and lame of the neighbourhood."* But this only applied to meat from *"those deer that are not sweete, nor meete to be eaten of the best sort of people."* (*Worcestershire Relics, John Noake, 1877*) Consequently the hungry relied mainly on the charity of the monks to provide for their daily needs and a community of the poor gradually collected around Great Malvern Priory. James Nott wrote

Great Malvern Priory and Gateway by J. Cooper, published in 1787.

that after the closure of the monastery *"None mourned its fall more than the neighbouring poor"*.

During the Dissolution of the Monasteries by Henry VIII in the 16th century, across the country carved effigies were smashed and church treasures, revenues and

BENEDICTINE MONK.

possessions were confiscated by the crown. Unlike some other monasteries, by then the Benedictine Priory at Malvern was not considered to be corrupt and Bishop Latimer pleaded unsuccessfully for it to be spared, saying that the Prior was *"an honest man and a good house-keeper; he feedeth many and that daily, for the country is poor and full of penury"*. However, the monastery accommodation and cloisters were destroyed, the Priory records lost, and the priors and monks were scattered from Malvern in 1539. By the time Henry's daughter Elizabeth I came to the throne, ownership of the humble donkey had spread widely beyond the Roman Catholic clergy to the general population of Britain. W. J. Gordon writing in 'The Horse World of London' in 1893 said *"Donkeys made an appearance amongst us in the days of Elizabeth, when they first became common in these islands"*.

Many ordinary people now used the donkey as a beast of burden because of its adaptability and usefulness for both travel and trade. Not only were they regarded as being practical steeds, but at that time donkeys were themselves believed to be an actual aid to healing, which would have brought added comfort to Malvern's sickly

visitors. As well as carrying Jesus into Jerusalem, a donkey was also said to have offered to carry Christ's cross and donkeys were believed to still bear its shadow on their backs as a sign of blessing. In medieval Worcestershire and Herefordshire this dark cross was thought to have supernatural powers, as was the light cross on hot-cross buns made from consecrated dough at Easter. *"The superstitious frequently preserved Good Friday buns from year to year, from the belief of their efficacies in curing diseases."*

(Notes and Queries for Worcestershire, John Noake 1856)

At Staunton-on-Wye in Herefordshire, mothers plucked and plaited the dark hairs from the cross on the donkey's back into a necklace strung around a baby's neck to prevent teething pains. A cure for whooping cough in the parish of Almeley was to pluck two hairs and place them under the bark of

When shall we three meet again.

Late 19th century donkey postcard with superstitious overtones, where a central mirror reflects the viewers image.

a 'Sally Tree', usually oak or ash, while in Malvern a child was passed three times over a donkeys back to achieve a cure. In the 19th century some local people still wore these hairs in a tiny silk bag around their necks as a magical protection against fits, convulsions and even miscarriage. One old Worcestershire superstition read *"To place a child on the dark cross on the donkey's back is sure to do him good"*. (Worcestershire Book, Federation of Women's Institutes, 1932) Belief in these healing powers would have made donkeys appropriate mounts for the weak and infirm visiting the holy wells in medieval Malvern.

The frail and ill would have had to make their difficult journeys here on ponies, mules or donkeys, as in the medieval period the Malvern Forest was marshy, densely wooded, and contained wild boar and wolves. Inevitably some of the sickliest patients did not survive their visit here. Later, in just one year in the 17th century, the Great Malvern Priory Register recorded three entries of people who visited the Holy Well *"and there died, these being the earliest original references to Malvern as a health resort. We know that the diseased were then coming in large numbers."* (Malvern Priory Registers, F.C.Morgan, 1924)

The Devils Oak, a misshapen tree in Malvern Forest. Edwin Lees, 1877.

*"Died 1612. A stranger died at ye holeie well.
A pore man from the holeie well.
A stranger 7th Sep. came to holi-well from srobrie (Shrewsbury)."*

But remarkable cures have been attributed to Malvern's holy waters since at least the 12th century and research by Dr Nash in the 18th century records that the spring at the Holy Well had been *"long used with great success, particularly in disorders of the eyes, scrophulos cases, old ulcers, leprosies and other diseases of the skin"*. A long poem written by *"J.M., gentleman."* at the end of the 16th century entitled *"The Newe Notamorphosie"*, provides an early written testament to the fame of the healing power of *"Malvern-hilles-well"*, interpreted to mean the Holy Well. This gentleman, being in ill health, had been sent by his doctors to try various medicinal springs and so he came to the Malverns, where *"he derived considerable benefit from the water."* (*Berrow's Journal, January 1921*)

> *"But at that tyme there was wondrous fame*
> *Of Malverne-hilles-well, for that bare the name.*
> *For medi'cynable virtues from them all*
> *Twixt both the Malvernes it from a hill doth fall.*
> *Here I staid longer, that I might thereby*
> *Experience learne, and the waters' virtues try.*
> *Cures of some it did, both many and great.*
> *It drew greate concourse to that pleasant Seate."*
> (*J.M., gentleman, 1600, British Museum*)

On the rediscovery of this poem in the 20th century a local newspaper reported, *"We are perhaps, too much accustomed to think of Malvern's reputation beginning in the 18th century, and it is interesting to find that it was a popular health resort as early as the time*

Holy Well building, with panniers for carrying bottled water c1870.

of Elizabeth. And I think we may be sure that the virtue of the water was not a discovery of the Elizabethan age. The very name Holy Well suggests that it was given in the Middle Ages." (*Berrow's Journal, January 1921*)

The Holy Well was sufficiently valued for it to be given as a reward to John Hornyold in 1558 by Queen Elizabeth I and it was still in his family's ownership in 1919. As the healing properties of Malvern's holy wells were evidently sought after in Elizabethan England, donkeys would not only have been used to carry the weakest patients up to them but also as pack animals to transport quantities of water from the wells down the steep hillsides to the main tracks. On the 31st May 1557, Roger Willis a *"water berer"* was buried in Malvern. Mr Morgan the local librarian said, *"It is well known that in all medieval towns a water bearer or water leader was a common feature, but it does not seem that one should be necessary in the village of Malvern in the middle of the 16th century, unless he was occupied in taking our pure water to places at a distance"*.

Watercolour of "A donkey stand near Malvern Wells Church" by Mary Brandling 1856. Courtesy of Malvern Library.

During a severe national drought in 1615, news that Malvern's springs were still flowing spread across the country and at about this time demand was such that an *"ancient dame"* on horseback was transporting the water in bottles from Ditchford Well on the lower slopes, to Worcester. This is the earliest known mention of Malvern water being bottled. According to a poem published in Bannister's 'Breviary of the Eye', by 1622 thousands of bottles were being filled at Malvern's holy wells and widely distributed. It is likely that donkeys with panniers would have had to be used to carefully carry so many bottles of water down the steep hillside slopes from the higher springs.

> *"A thousand bottles here, were filled weekly,*
> *And many costrils rare, for stomachs sickly;*
> *Some were to London sent,*
> *Some of them into Kent,*
> *Others on to Berwick went,   O praise the Lord."*

One of the first named 'water-cure' patients is recorded as travelling here from Worcester, eight miles away. She was Mary Maunsell, a lame woman who set out in 1672 "to goe to Malverne Well in hope of some benefit by that water." (*May's Guide to Malvern 1886*) but how she travelled here is not recorded. As the fame of the holy waters spread further, more and more needy people came to these spring sources believing in their healing powers, and before the end of the 17th century the waters were even sought after in fashionable circles for ladies *"to wash their faces and make 'em fair."*

Hymn in Praise of Malvern

Edmund Rea

Great Malvern on a rock, thou standest surely;
Do not thyself forget, living securely;
Thou hast of blessings store,
No country town hath more,
Do not forget therefore,
>   To praise the Lord.

Out of thy famous hill, there daily springeth
A water, passing still, which always bringeth
Great comfort to all them
That are diseased men,
And makes them well again,
>   To praise the Lord.

Hast thou a wound to heal, the which doth grieve thee?
Come then unto this well, it will relieve thee;
'Noli me tangeres',
And other maladies,
Here have their remedies,
>   Prais'd be the Lord.

(Three of sixteen verses attributed to the Vicar of Malvern between 1612 – 1640)

4 - Distillation, Development and Donkeys

By the 13th century much of the land of the royal forest had become the 'Malvern Chase' given by Edward I to his son-in-law the Earl of Gloucester, but the district was still strictly controlled, although now *"it at once changed both name and character, and became more under control of common law."* (*Worcestershire Relics, John Noake, 1877*) Each local parish became responsible for the care and sustenance of the needy, which was costly, so destitute or sickly migrants and *"wanderers"* from another parish were often whipped and driven out, or forcibly returned to their parish of origin. From 1556 to 1617 not only were many deaths of wandering men and women recorded in Great Malvern, but also during these years many babies were registered as being born, baptised and dying on the same day. The real poverty of many of those attracted by the holy wells suggests that they would have travelled here either on foot or, if they were very weak, on humble donkeys. The birth statistics in the Priory Register for this period were summarised as, *"The burials of children form a very large proportion of the total entries. Out of 31 deaths in 1607 seventeen were of children, many other years were as bad. ... Illegitimate births number 68 and in addition twenty-three children of vagrants, or wandering, or strange women, as they are variously called, saw the light first in Malvern."* (*Malvern Priory Registers, F.C.Morgan, 1924*) There were as yet no workhouses where these *"poor unfortunates"* could be cared for so the entry for the birth of these babies frequently read *"born in a barne"*.

In the 17th century the inhabitants of two thirds of the Chase were given 'commoners rights' to collect windfall wood and graze a few animals on the 'uninclosed' land. By the 18th century the better off Malvern residents derived their domestic water from their own private wells beside their houses, while impoverished inhabitants, sickly visitors and wanderers still had to collect water from the hillside springs. It seems that some of the poorer families began to make a meagre living by hiring out their donkeys as transport to carry both passengers and water to and from these high springs and wells. From the 18th century onwards until the beginning of the 20th century, there are increasing records for the popularity of hire-donkeys on the hills and commons.

Describing various means of transport in his Guide to Malvern published in 1895, Charles Grindrod wrote of the hill donkeys, *"the most famous and time-honoured of all, – it is to be feared not always hide-honoured – are the donkeys. These useful little animals have since the dawn of modern Malvern been associated with the place and can always be hired for ascending the hills at a price*

Hire-donkeys ridden on Link Common in 1858. Etching by Rock & Co.

as modest as themselves, several 'stands' being close above the town, with boys and women waiting eager for orders".

The beginnings of 'modern' Malvern can be traced back to the results of the early scientific work of Dr John Wall. When treating his patients at Worcester Infirmary in the 1750s, Dr Wall analysed the waters of several of Malvern's springs by distillation, particularly the Chalybeate (iron) Spring in Great Malvern, the Holy Well and Eye Well in Malvern Wells. The purity of the latter pair helped him to develop the recipe for English bone china, named Royal Worcester Porcelain by

Early stereoscopic photograph of a donkey station on Wells Common, c1845, probably by Francis Bedford.

King George III during his visit in 1788. The profits from Dr Wall's book *"Experiments and Observations on the Malvern Water"* first published *"without a name"* in 1754, and then again in 1757 and 1769, were *"devoted to assisting the many needy sick who came*

Dr John Wall, 1708 - 1776.

for treatment". (F.C. Morgan, Public Librarian, Malvern c.1930) The first public subscription list for donations towards providing accommodation near the Holy Well was opened in September 1754. In his observations *"Several cases were described to prove the efficacy of the waters. They speak of weary treks by the sick and the lame through the pretty hillside village to the steep slopes beyond. There, at the well-side, their faith was rewarded and their limbs refreshed. One lady was quite blind when she was led to the well, but she so far improved that she was able to see a flea jumping on her bed". (The History of the Worcester Royal Infirmary, William H. McMenemey, 1947)*

At a time when the level of the unpleasant taste of minerals in waters was believed to signify their power to heal, Dr Wall promoted the unusually clean taste and purity of

Probably the first permanent well house at Holy Well built in the late 18th century.

The present Holy Well built in 1843, which seems to incorporate the ground floor of the former well house. Etching by Newman 1848.

Malvern water as its healing power. He also raised subscriptions from the gentry to make the springs *"more commodious"*, *"putting them in order"* by building wooden huts as baths beside several, where an individual patient could bathe their afflicted parts more discreetly. All these developments attracted a higher class of invalid, with many more wealthy people now coming here to take the waters, but the weakest of these patients would still have had to be carried up the steepest hill tracks to the springs on sure-footed donkeys. In 1763 the Duke of York visited the Holy Well, commenting on *"the remarkable efficacy of the waters"*, after which its popularity with the gentry was assured. A succession of temporary bath-houses were built at the Holy Well but the first permanent building over the site was not recorded until 1815, as *"a seemly building consisting of a bath and several apartments"*. After this animals had to be watered separately at the public spout behind the well house.

The Eye Well was once a much more prolific source, but was damaged when a villager with a pick-axe tried to divert the supply to his cottage in the 19th century.

View down the steep slope from the Eye Well to the back of Holy Well c1900.

From the 1760s Malvern Wells became the favourite water cure destination for the gentry. Not only was the village closest to the ancient Holy Well and the Eye Well, but also accommodation now became available at the Admiral Benbow, the Essington Hotel, and in larger and more elegant houses than presently existed in the other little villages, including Great Malvern. But entertainments here were very few outside the social gatherings in these boarding houses, except for hill climbs and regular donkey and pony races on a flat track across Wells Common. A hundred years later in 1854 the spoil, dug out from the new railway tunnel through the hills, was used to widen this area into the broad grassy drive that exists today. In 1862 Cuthbert Bede recommended that mothers who *"consider the steepness of the hills to be fraught with danger"*, should send their children *"out upon the Link common, or to the uninclosed chase between Great Malvern and Malvern Wells, where fresh air and donkey rides can be simultaneously enjoyed".* C.F. Severn Burrow remembered that in her 19th century childhood this drive was called 'The Gallop' and was still used *"for the exercising of horses and the joy of children, where we rode our donkeys and arranged running and jumping contests".*

Great Malvern also became a regular destination as visitor numbers increased, but at first the only accommodation was in the 17th century Abbey boarding

Elegant houses at Malvern Wells, by Newman & Co., 1874.

house or in neighbouring farmhouses and the few cottages. Dr Benjamin Stillingfleet's description, written in a letter of 1757, indicates the impact of these early water cure visitors on Great Malvern. *"I have been in Malvern about twelve days, where, with difficulty, I have got lodgings, the place is so full, nor do I wonder at it, there being some instances of very extraordinary cures, in cases looked on as desperate, even by Dr Wall, who first brought these waters into vogue. I do not doubt that the air and exercise, which at present is absolutely necessary here, the well being about two miles from the town, contribute very much towards restoring the health of the patients. The road is very fine, and made on purpose for the convenience of the drinkers."*

As well as the development of better roads, from at least 1807 onwards better hill pathways, terraces and bridle paths were made by 'the great and the good' people

Walks, bridle paths and viewing terraces on the summit of the Beacon looking south, 1877.

who had been attracted here by the springs. These philanthropic Lords and Ladies, Countesses, Clergymen and Generals paid for these improvements to make *"exercise on the hills easier both on foot and by the donkeys, which were popular in the town before 1817"*. (*A History of Malvern, Brian Smith, 1964*) Hotelkeepers and other businessmen now saw the numerous visitors to the new walks and bridle paths around St Ann's Well as an opportunity for the development of Great Malvern rather than Malvern Wells. In 1796 the old school building became the Crown Inn where the annual venison feast was held, *"the oldest house for general accommodation in the village"*, originally on the site of Lloyds Bank, Belle Vue Terrace. Horse-drawn mail coaches would deliver passengers here from Piccadilly in London, a journey that took thirty hours to complete. Donkeys could then be hired nearby to explore around the hills and up the new steep trackways to St Ann's Well.

"During the early years of the 19th century more and more had resorted to Great Malvern for various complaints." (*Malvern In and Near, Stevens & Co, 1904*) Among the early visitors was the lame Lord Byron, who came to Malvern with his mother in 1801, aged 13, probably for treatment to his deformed foot. He later recalled in his diary the deep impression that the Worcestershire Beacon had made on him. *"I can never forget the effect, a few years afterwards in England, of the only thing I had seen, even in miniature, of a mountain, in the Malvern Hills. After I had returned to Cheltenham, I used to watch it every afternoon at sunset, with a sensation which I cannot describe."* In 1808 he wrote of staying here for longer. *"I spent the summer vacation of the year on the Malvern Hills; those were days of romance."* Byron is referring here to the romance of the natural landscape, the growing search for the 'picturesque' emphasised by the Romantic Movement in literature and the arts, qualities identified and published by Reverend William Gilpin in 1782. J.M.W. Turner visited Great Malvern in this early period, painting two romantic views of the Priory Gateway in 1795. In 1832 Elizabeth Barrett Browning, crippled by a fall from her pony, visited *"the rocky passage"* of the Wyche Pass and wrote, *"I looked on each side of the elevated place where I sat. Herefordshire all hill and wood – undulating*

"Malvern Priory Gateway" in a lightening storm, J.M.W. Turner, 1795.

and broken – Worcestershire throwing out a great unbroken prospect, and more than Worcestershire, to the horizon. One prospect attracting the eye by picturesqueness; the other the mind, the sublimity."

A donkey waiting near a grocery stall at the Priory Gateway, beside Crown Inn stables. Lithograph 1856.

Donkeys arriving at St Ann's Well cottage built in 1815. Etching published by Rock & Co. 1850.

As well as the springs, the little village of Great Malvern was now also attracting cultured visitors and new residents seeking life in idyllic rural landscapes away from the noise and grime of industrialisation. By 1816 the village consisted of *"about 50 houses, chiefly neat buildings, to which are attached gardens and plantations of fruit, trees, shrubs and evergreens"*. Of these *"twenty two were lodging houses, Tradesmen's and houses of entertainment"* including the Unicorn Inn and the Belle Vue Hotel with its stables at the rear and a main carriage entrance, now an arcade. *"About the spots occupied by these Hotels, the owners of Jerusalem ponies ply for hire: here are also to be let, Donkey carts, where the patrons of the whip may drive these animals curricle or tandem."* (*A General History of Malvern, John Chambers 1817*)

John Downs built the Downs' Hotel in 1810, which he soon renamed the Foley Arms in honour of the Lords of the Manor. By the 1820s Great Malvern's popularity was even more assured following the creation of the Library, and then the Coburg Baths and Pump Room next door, directly opposite the Unicorn Inn with its central donkey stand.   The Library was run by John Southall the Priory organist and his wife Mary, with accommodation and board costing the princely sum of two guineas a week, while

a labourer's wage was just three shillings and six pence. The elegant library building with its bow-fronted corner provided a social and cultural centre holding assemblies, conferences, balls and weekly *"Routs"* or parties. It also contained other attractions to entertain middle and upper class visitors; a reading room with newspapers, a music room, a billiard room and 'the Bazaar' selling souvenirs, including some early prints by Lamb of the donkey rides, as well as *"snuff, patent medicines, stationery and a few other articles likely to attract the fancy"*.

Detail of a picturesque view of the village showing Belle Vue Terrace and the Library. Watercolour by William Wells 1830.

From the mid 18th to the early 19th centuries this influx of the gentry, in search of the picturesque and also to 'take the waters', had resulted in the first wave of development of Great Malvern from a series of hillside dwellings into a small spa health resort providing entertainments, with

Early photo of the Belle Vue Hotel and Library, c1855.

carriage excursions and hillside donkey rides to visit the springs and see the 'romantic' views.

One later 'water-curist' found that the best vantage points had become so familiar to his donkey that *"if left to itself, it would always stand still when it came to the most attractive points of view. I don't pretend, of course, to say that an ass has any natural taste in landscape, but the custom of those who ride them to pull up at beautiful and taking prospects, has habituated the creatures to pause at these particular points, as much as to say 'there's a view for you'."* (*Three Weeks in Wet Sheets by a Moist Visitor 1851*)

But as early as 1824 the growing number of donkeys were beginning to cause a nuisance and a complaint was recorded of *"great damage … done to the young trees planted for the sake of ornament on part of Malvern Hill by Donkeys being turned thereon by Persons having no right to do so. And also great inconvenience arises to the Public by a great number of Donkeys for hire being placed in the middle of the Highway in the height of the Malvern Summer Season."* (*Malvern Hills Conservators' Archive, Malvern Chase, Pamela Hurle, 2007*)

From this 'modern' period onwards the growing fame of the donkey-hire trade in the Malverns is inseparable from the growth of the water cure and the town itself, with stands at numerous springs, spouts, hotels and boarding houses around the Malvern Hills. For over a hundred and fifty years donkeys were plied for hire to the adventurous in search of beautiful landscape views, as well as to the sick or infirm seeking the healing waters.

Romantic watercolour of the Worcestershire landscape with a donkey boy resting on the Malvern Hills, Mary Brandling 1856. Courtesy of Malvern Library.

Holy Well

Hydropota

Oh Malvern, never envy thou
  the springs enroled by fame
since Walls ingenious pen has now
  immortalised thy name.

Henceforth shall rapturous poets sing
  of Helicon no more;
the waters of thy purer spring
  can boast superior power.

We too of inspiration tell,
  as bards who drink shall feel,
the streams from Malvern's holy well
  can both inspire and heal.

(May 1755)

5 - The Pauper and the Princess

The popularity of the donkey rides was widely publicised when the Illustrated London News published an engraving of the busy scene at one donkey stand in an article by Cuthbert Bede in 1856. *"The chief of these donkey stations is situated a little below St Ann's Well; the zigzag road was made for her Majesty, when, as Princess Victoria, she visited Malvern and ascended the hill. … Just at this spot by the donkey station, it is shaded by trees, under whose dappled shadows it is pleasant to linger on a fierce July day."*

An engraving of the popular donkey stand on the zig-zag route to St. Ann's Well was first published by the Illustrated London News in 1856. This coloured version of the same view was sold as a souvenir in 1858.

Donkeys were regarded as the safest means of passenger transport up the hill slopes and consequently were much favoured by ladies and children. One old saying was *"Better to ride on a donkey that carries me home than a horse that throws me"*. Grindrod said, *"The donkeys are useful appendages in ascending the hills, being very sure-footed; indeed they are so perfectly safe that in twelve years we do not recollect one accident occasioned by a donkey."* Many of Malvern's visitors came from London where they were familiar with donkeys being used mainly by poor costermongers as pack animals in commerce, not as a means of transport for the gentry. At the turn of the century, Dorothy Hartley recalled the carefulness and reliability of the costermongers' donkeys in the East End. *"There were rows of country-type cottages with shut-in gardens at their backs and the costers' donkeys lived there behind the cottages and you could watch them in the morning coming out through the front doors; picking their way, neat-footed, over the babies playing in the narrow passage. … They were very sociable and reliable donkeys."* (Leana Pooley, Covent Garden Area Trust 2007)

Local people in Malvern had some affection for the hill donkeys and some still fondly recount the story of 'Old Moses', a donkey owned by Betty Keelay, Keeley or Caley, born c1770, who carried Princess Victoria safely up to St Ann's Well in the early 19th century. The publicity created by this royal ride by the future Queen made Malvern a most elegant and fashionable resort, attracting famous and well-to-do visitors twelve years before the expensive private water cure treatments of Dr Wilson and Dr Gully had begun.

"Betty Keelay" born c1770, with her companion pony and donkey, watercolour c1830. Courtesy of Malvern Library.

46

Victoria was born on 24th May 1819 and had a *"rather melancholy childhood"*, her father dying only eight months later. The last legitimate heir to the throne had died in infancy in 1821, the daughter of her uncle and aunt, the future King William IV and Queen Adelaide, but his many illegitimate children by his mistress Mrs Jordan still survived, causing tensions in the royal family. Victoria's late father had also openly kept a mistress and her mother now decided that they would not attend William's coronation. To avoid any hint of scandal the eleven-year-old Victoria was then isolated from any *"contaminating influence"* of the Royal Court by her uncle Leopold who was trying to establish a rival Court around her. By 1830 it was clear that the little Princess would succeed the King, so her mother began taking the new heir to the throne on tours to see the country

A satirical cartoon by William Heath in 1830, the year that the child came to stay in Malvern, shows Victoria sitting on her uncle Leopold's knee as he grooms her for the monarchy.

she was going to rule and they came to visit Great Malvern and the hills.

The Duchess of Kent brought the young Princess *"to stay at Holly Mount Cottage for several months. Here the child rambled freely in the woods and on the hills, and rode often on the donkeys, especially her favourite Moses, who thereafter was called the 'Royal Moses', attended by the donkey-woman in a bonnet and red cloak. ... She*

The original head-band of "The Royal Moses". Courtesy of Malvern Museum.

"D'ye want a nice donkey for the little lady, Mam?" This polite title implies that the donkey is being hired by Princess Victoria and her mother. Undated etching by Cuthbert Bede, sold at the Library before it became 'Royal'.

After these royal visits the prefix 'Royal' was emblazoned above the Library, photo c. 1880

performed here what was probably her first public function by declaring open a new path made near St Ann's Well, from Nob's Delight to the Foley Walk." (*A Little City set on a Hill by C.F. Severn Burrow 1948*)   This excursion made donkey riding extremely popular here and from then on the road that zigzags to the well house and on up to the summit of the Beacon was known as Victoria Drive and the road to Holly Mount Cottage became Queen's Drive.   During her ten-week stay Victoria also visited the Bazaar in the library building, which then became the 'Royal' Library.   In 'Malvern Country' Vincent Waite writes, *"For many years one of the Malvern Donkeys bore a badge of distinction on its bridle and was given the name 'Royal' Moses as a reward for carrying the future Queen of England up to the top of Worcestershire Beacon.   But the recollection of the Duchess of Kent's ample figure prompts the thought that it was her donkey which should have received the grateful reward rather than Moses, who after all, was carrying only a small eleven-year-old child."*

However Charles Grindrod recorded that, when living at Great Witley Court from 1844 onwards, the now widowed Queen Adelaide often visited Malvern and also enjoyed riding the hills on Moses.   In 1856 Cuthbert Bede gave a more detailed account, reporting that the Queen *"was not content with paying in gold for a ride to St Ann's Well, but further inquired of the donkey woman what she could do to serve her.   'Please, your Majesty, give a name to my donkey,' replied the woman whose earthly wishes appear to have been limited. So her Majesty did what, perhaps,* other Majesties had been graciously pleased to condescend to do before her - she gave a name to a donkey, and 'Moses' was henceforth known as 'the Royal Moses.'"

In the earliest known report in 1851, Joseph Leech wrote that Queen Adelaide had ridden Moses from the back entrance of the Foley Arms up to the well and had paid his owner *"a guinea and a half – the smaller sum for the use of the quadruped, and the larger one for the encouragement of the owner"*. After this honour Granny Keeley asked if she could now call him *"the Royal Moses"*. Queen Adelaide smiled and replied that *"she had no objection to the old woman calling her donkey what she liked. A new forehead band was accordingly embroidered for the illustrious ass, and 'Royal Moses' stood for the future upon the Donkey 'Change without a compeer. The incident was nevertheless the origin of fortune in a small way to the politic old woman. All the young and old lady visitors to Malvern were anxious to be able to say on their return that they had ridden the same quadruped as the Queen Dowager."* Cuthbert Bede was told that later *"the good Queen Adelaide sent her donkey-driver a handsome whip, and that the old woman made 'a nice mess of money' and took it with her to Worcester, where*

A busy donkey scene at the start of Victoria Drive, by Cuthbert Bede 1861. Courtesy of Database of Mid-Victorian Wood-Engraved Illustration, Cardiff University.

Malvern, Road Leading to St Ann's Well

Postcard of same view photographed in the 1890s.

Betty Keeley and her donkey team, by Cuthbert Bede published in 1861. Courtesy of Database of Mid-Victorian Wood-Engraved Illustration, Cardiff University.

she lived and died in genteel retirement". The census records three generations of Elizabeth (Betty) Keeley born from c1770 to 1837, who had all lived on the common of Malvern Chase.

By all accounts the old donkey had *"very soon died of a surfeit of Royalty, for he was so patronised that he was fairly ridden to death"*, yet he was then portrayed as an aging donkey affectionately called "Old Moses" in an etching published by Rock and Co. in 1855, presumably as a commemorative portrait. After his death many of the local donkeys were renamed 'Royal' in his memory, but some say this was only to try to attract more customers. *"His progeny appears to have been a numerous one, and to have individually enjoyed the royal prefix bestowed upon the illustrious head of the family. … Not only do we meet with 'the Royal Joshua' and 'Royal Abraham' but also with 'the Royal Polly' and 'the Royal Dick'. … The names of the donkeys afford no small amusement to their juvenile riders, who may be heard freely discussing the relative paces and speed of their respective royally entitled animals."* (*Illustrated London News, Cuthbert Bede, 1856*)

It seems that those visitors who stayed for the summer season often hired their favourite donkey for the whole period. Bede writes that on leaving Malvern one *"cured"* invalid suggested to a lady friend that she take on her reliable donkey, but the nervous lady first tried to make further enquiries.

St Ann's Well cottage and the bath-house opened in 1820, with donkey riders above and below.

50

OLD MOSES.

"Before going away she recommended me a donkey, which she has used for several months. The animal, she assures me, is a most gentle creature, and the boy attentive and respectful. Now I have been very unfortunate hereto in my donkeys, and should be glad to secure the services of this; so should you go up to the village, just quietly try to ascertain the character of 'Royal Dick'."

Even more visitors were now using donkeys to reach St Ann's Well cottage, which was then extended with the new octagon built in about 1860. The donkeys were watered at a separate spring outlet that was just beside the well room entrance and this was still flowing with water until the 1990s. At my suggestion this source was newly named "Old Moses Spout" by Anne Jenkins of the Heritage Lottery Fund, in memory of this once famous donkey. The site was restored in 2005 and an animal trough and cascade added to the spout in a unique partnership between the Malvern Spa Association, the local

Donkeys for hire at St Ann's Well cottage and new octagon, with the side spout where they were watered in the background, c1865.

Emily the donkey stands patiently nearby as David Armitage of The Malvern Hills Area of Outstanding Natural Beauty speaks at the naming of "Old Moses' Spout", St Ann's Well, following the restoration of the pond and side spout, December 2005.

Area of Outstanding Natural Beauty office, the Malvern Hills Conservators who own the well and land and the Heritage Lottery Fund. Although a respected dowser traced the original water source to high in the valley above, permission to dig there and unblock the pipe was refused. The outlet spout is now intermittently supplied by pump from the well behind St Ann's cottage. At the official opening the waters were blessed by Reverend John Barr from Great Malvern Priory while a donkey called Emily stood patiently by to remind us of the historic role of these hard-working animals at St Ann's Well. But to everyone's amusement, she stubbornly refused to drink from 'Old Moses Spout', reminding us that you can lead a donkey to water, but you can't make it drink.

But Queen Victoria evidently retained a taste for Malvern water and under great security the Burrows brothers supplied the royal family with table water from a secret spring above Great Malvern, probably until as late as the 1950s. Allan Knight told me of his father being sworn to secrecy about its location during his first job as a boy at W. & J. Burrows' Bottling Works. *"His first task of the week was to climb the hills at seven in the morning with a carry bag with six glass flasks, always accompanied by an adult. Somewhere high on the side of the hill above Rose Bank House, beyond St Ann's Well was a steel door that was unlocked to reveal the spring, which served the bottling plant. He would fill each flask with water and carry it back to the plant on Belle Vue Terrace. Each batch delivered had to be certified pure. These flasks were sent to Bristol to be tested for purity, to comply with new regulations, before the bottled water could be transported to the royal family. This was around 1937."* (Mr A. Knight 2006)

Today Coca-Cola supply bottled Malvern water to the royal household from the Pewtriss Spring, now known as Primeswell, piped to the old Schweppes bottling plant in Colwall. As well as Malvern water, Queen Victoria also retained her liking for donkeys throughout her life and during a visit to Aix-les-Baines in 1887, her Jubilee year, a national newspaper reported that she was still *"fond of driving out in a small carriage drawn by a donkey. Usually it is the Princess Beatrice who drives"*.

Holly Mount with Princess Victoria riding a donkey. "Drawing made during the Royal visit", 1830.

Example of a little donkey carriage from the Victorian period.

In Praise of Malvern's Air and Water

(anonymous, May 1776)

Ye nymphs, oppressed by Worcester's stagnant air
To Malvern's high aerial walks repair,
Where springs, and gales, their mutual aid dispense,
To purge the blood and quicken every sense;
Here the pale face its former tint resumes,
And every charm with fresher beauty blooms;
Haste then, ye nymphs and range awhile at large,
So shall ye save for paint an annual charge.

(Written on a pane of glass at Malvern Wells)

6 - Fame, Fortune and Regulation

After Victoria's visit to Malvern generous benefactors erected more accessible public spouts for the use of the less fortunate poor and visitors, including the prolific spout in Spring Lane, Malvern Link, created by Lord Sandy in about 1835, and the North Malvern Tank spout, Lower Wyche Spout and West Malvern Tap, all built by Charles Morris between 1835 - 1844. Most of the poorer residents relied on these spouts as their sole supply of fresh water for the household and for their animals. Donkeys could now also be hired from impoverished women at several of these new outlets as cheap and reliable local transport, probably to carry water.

Lord Sandy's Spout. Artist's proposal for new pillars and pathway to help identify the hidden site from Spring Lane, by Rose Garrard 2004.

Lord Sandy's Spout after restoration with new pillars and pathway as part of the Malvern Heritage Project, 2008.

Group of donkey women stationed at one of the two Morris spouts that have high curved walls. Said to be Betty Keeley (born in 1814) and Moses, on left.

The same scene on a stereoscopic card, probably by Francis Bedford. Etchings were often based on these early photographs c1850.

The Doctors James Wilson and James Manby Gully brought the practice of hydro-therapy to Great Malvern from Priessnitz in Austria, opening the first commercial water cure establishments in Great Malvern from 1842 onwards, to exploit the town's existing springs and wells. Throughout the following thirty years the population increased even more rapidly as many well-to-do new residents, visitors and patients were attracted to Great Malvern, now known as "the Metropolis of the Water Cure". They hoped to improve their health by taking the waters under the strict guidance of the growing

Busy Belle Vue Terrace, Great Malvern, published by Newman & Co., 1876.

multitude of expensive private water cure doctors, whose portraits were often hung as advertisements in the shop windows and inns. Malvern was prospering and it was said that, *"You only have to put out a bucket and gold sovereigns rain into it"*. In the 1840s a manual labourer earned about sixpence a day, but one week of the water cure cost about five pounds, over thirty times a workingman's wage, although Dr Wilson did give concessions to poorer patients. For only a few pennies these elegant ladies, gentlemen and small children, as well as the sick and elderly invalids, frequently hired donkeys to carry them up the steep slopes to drink at the healing springs.

Rare photo of an early Victorian group riding donkeys on the Malvern Hills, with two donkey boys.

Malvern was now the fashionable health resort of the intelligentsia, favoured by many renowned politicians, scholars, poets and writers. *"Charles Dickens spent some time at Malvern early in the fifties. The place was then the sole resort of hydropathy in England. Dr Gully was in the zenith of his fame; and Wilson's large establishment, and almost every lodging house in Malvern, was full of water patients."* (*Malvern Priory Church, James Nott, 1895*)

"Going Uphill, Malvern" etching published by Lamb and sold at the Royal Library, c1840.

In 'Household Words', a weekly journal edited by Dickens, he recorded his observations of the excitement, perils and fun of climbing the hills on foot and by donkey. *"The slipperiness of the grass on these slopes seems really worse than ice. As we sit under a bank, eating our dinner, we see two young ladies on an opposite slope in an almost helpless position. They can make no way, upwards or sideways, with feet, knees or hands. There is nothing to grasp and the grass is shiny as*

Popular way of "Going down hill", Malvern, 1853.

satin. If they join hands, they go down only the faster. ... For some time, as we walked southwards along the ridge, the grass has been growing thinner and now we have really rough walking on broken rock. There is an adventurous lady on her donkey, at such a height, on such a ridge, among this debris. What is her child asking, that toddling two year old? 'Who made all this mess?' My dear little fellow, what an irreverent question! He will not find that out for his mother cannot answer him for laughing."

In the 1850s the town's many famous visitors also included Wordsworth, Tennyson, Gladstone, Disraeli, Carlyle, Thomas Macaulay, Florence Nightingale who was convalescing here after the Crimean War, and Charles Darwin, who was searching for a cure for the severe gastric ailments he had suffered since his voyage on the Beagle. Already considered an atheist, he became even more disillusioned with the idea of God after his favourite but sickly ten year old daughter died at Montreal House in 1851 whilst also a patient of Dr Gully. Little Annie, *"a dear and good child"* is modestly buried beside a tree in the Priory Churchyard. Knowing it would cause great controversy amongst Christians, it was not until eight years later that Darwin decided to publish 'The Origin of the Species', his influential theory of evolution.

But the popularity of the little village brought rapid changes and in 1851 it officially became a town. That same year Joseph Leech climbed up to the top of the Worcestershire Beacon and reported, *"Romantic as the view is, I defy you to be very romantic here, for the moment you place your foot on the summit commerce cries and clatters around you with its importunate clamour in the shape of basket girls pestering you to become the purchaser of ginger beer, biscuits and walnuts, or the*

Basket seller and her donkey team pestering a gentleman on the summit of the Beacon, c1900.

owners of return donkeys tempting you with cheap rides down again." (*Three Weeks in Wet Sheets by a Moist Visitor, 1851*)

As well as the busy scene on the Beacon he also described the growing size of the main donkey stand in the town centre. *"The 'Donkey Change' is not far from the Bazaar, and here may be found at times as many as forty or fifty of these patient creatures accoutred and ready for work, the majority being equipped for ladies, with white cotton cloths covering the side saddles. Each animal has its name embroidered across the forehead band, and the ingenuity displayed by the owners in giving them names, most of which betoken beauty and sprightliness, is very entertaining."*

At the height of the water cure there were at least ten private donkey 'stands' in Great Malvern alone, where dozens of donkeys would wait for hire to carry people to St Ann's Well, or on up to the summit of the Beacon and along the ridge of the hills. There were also seventeen Hackney carriage stands and many livery stables in the town for hire tours of the area by horse, pony, mule and donkey cart. This caused considerable congestion on the hill rides, as donkeys, ponies and horses vied for position on the pathways. *"As a rule, if the boy keeps up his work, the donkey does the same, and bores on steadily towards the top of the hill, pushing against his fellow donkeys, and expecting everybody to move out of his way. This pertinacity is far more likely to cause an accident than any lack of sure-footedness; and in July last, I saw two very narrow escapes. In one case a young lady was riding down the hill mounted upon a gay horse, when she encountered three female donkey-riders, whose donkeys were all abreast, and forced her off the path onto the steep and slippery hill side. … The other case was that of a gentleman who had driven to the top of the hill in a basket-carriage drawn by a pair of ponies, and on his way back was blocked by ascending donkeys, which caused such a to do and commotion, as I should fancy would be a warning to him never to repeat this experiment."* (*Leisure Hour, Malvern Donkeys, Cuthbert Bede, 1862*)

Hill donkey procession, published by Rock & Co., 1853.

The haphazard proliferation of these businesses encouraged the Malvern Commissioners to create a complex system of bylaws controlling the fair price of hire for the many carriages, horses, mules, donkeys and their drivers. *"The donkey drivers are* chiefly women and boys with a sprinkling of girls. ... No one is allowed the pleasure of becoming a donkey proprietor until she has obtained the consent of the Commissioners, and engaged to pay them an annual tribute of five shillings. When she has purchased the desired privilege she leads her donkey to his allotted station, and joins her brethren in their various cries of "Want a donkey, my lady?" "A nice donkey for the little girl, Ma'am?" "Nice side-saddle, Miss?" "Here's a donkey that'll just suit you, Sir!" (*Illustrated London News, Cuthbert Bede, 1856*)

"Want a donkey, Ma'am?" Touting for business at a hire stand with numerous donkeys. Etching by Cuthbert Bede 1856. Produced by Lamb and sold in the Royal Library,

As well as the central donkey-hire stand in the town beside the Unicorn Inn there were stands at some of the other inns and several on the routes leading to St Ann's Well, including a private stand at the top of the '99 Steps', now the garages in the grounds of Bello Sguardo. The stands on the hill were organised into two major donkey stations controlled by the Council, one on Victoria Drive and one at *"the entrance to the Winding Valley,* (now Happy Valley), *between the Beacon and the North Hill. At the hill stations there are sixty tax-paying donkeys, four licensed mules, and two ponies. Besides these there are mules and ponies kept in private stables in the town, and near to Victoria Drive; and other donkeys are stationed at the Link, Malvern Wells, and West Malvern."* (*Leisure Hour, Malvern Donkeys, Cuthbert Bede, 1862*)

A donkey carrying two children in panniers towards the Priory Gateway.

There were also private stables for the other main inns, the Foley, the Belle Vue Hotel and the Crown, whose stable building still exists beside the Priory Gateway, now occupied by First Paige printers. Even the magnificent refectory, the medieval timber Guesten Hall that was then on the other side of the Priory Gateway, *"had degraded*

"The Refectory of the Priory of Great Malvern". Etching by J. Basire, 1837.

into a barn and stable" before it was demolished in 1841 by William Archer, who began building the Abbey Hotel on the site in 1848. *"The donkeys are stabled during the night, and have a mouthful of hay; during the day they receive three feeds of oats, beans, bran and chaff; and after every journey they are indulged with a complimentary feed. On their way down from the hill-top they can also snatch a few minutes' browse on ferns and thymy grass; so that, on a busy day, they have as many feeds and snacks as a monthly nurse, and are kept well up to their work."* (Leisure Hour, Malvern Donkeys, Cuthbert Bede, 1862)

Group of donkeys with brass registration badges.

The quantity of animal droppings at all the stands in the streets caused concern so the Commissioners not only introduced licences but also appointed an official 'Scavenger' in 1852 to oversee the cleanliness and proper running of the donkey stations. *"The donkeys carry side saddles, whose antiquity or want of repair is judiciously concealed by a white cotton cloth. Every donkey-driver wears a numbered brass badge, and the donkeys have corresponding badges affixed to the front of their bridles, which are often decorated with rosettes, and almost invariably worked over with the donkey's name."* (Illustrated London News, Cuthbert Bede, 1856)

Donkeys for hire beside an unknown Malvern spout.
Watercolour by Mary Brandling 1856. Courtesy of Malvern
Library.

Detail showing an open fronted donkey shed in Happy Valley c1900.

The last surviving donkey stand structure in Happy Valley, 1997.

Early photo Happy Valley donkeys, c1850.

View down Happy Valley showing the Donkey Spout on the right. Detail of watercolour by A.R. Quinton 1913.

Often there was no actual 'stand' building but donkeys were just pitched for hire beside a road junction near a waterspout. The last surviving donkey stand structure was still in use until the 1940s. It was at the foot of Happy Valley in the ivy clad wooden hut that can still be seen today on the right at the top of St Ann's Road, now owned by the Malvern Hills Conservators.   Slightly further uphill beside the track on the left is a table-like structure, thought to have originally been a platform for loading and mounting donkeys to carry goods and people up to St Ann's Well.   Beneath it are the remains of a drinking spout and small animal trough where donkeys were watered and donkey-women collected water in pitchers to give to their thirsty clients.   The 'Donkey Spout' is also owned by the Conservators and is easily missed when the undergrowth is dense.

The Donkey Spout at the bottom of Happy Valley. Detail of lithograph by K.H. Lines, 1863.

The Prospect

Dr Nash

To the eastward we view Bosworth's gay plain,
Renowned by battle where King Richard was slain.
The flying fish too, we behold on Broadway Hill
from off the ascent of noble Malvern Hill.

Thus prospects anew on this hill be found,
You see at your leisure while viewing around
the waters much famed by Physicians of skill
that's found underneath Malvern's lofty high hill.

(Given by Lady Somers from Dr Nash's unpublished notes)

7 - Satire, Smoking and the Douche

The Crown was leased by both Dr Wilson and Dr Gully in 1842, renamed Graefenberg House and used to accommodate just twelve water cure patients with *"indefinite diseases which a large income and unbounded leisure are so well calculated to produce"*. These *"water-curists"* often began their day by imbibing water at Hay Well in the town centre before climbing by donkey to St Ann's Well and then proceeding onwards to other water sources. Early maps show that the prolific Hay Well used to be above a

THE
DANGERS OF THE WATER CURE
AND
ITS EFFICACY EXAMINED AND COMPARED
WITH THOSE OF THE
DRUG TREATMENT OF DISEASES,
AND AN
EXPLANATION OF ITS PRINCIPLES AND PRACTICE;
WITH AN ACCOUNT OF
CASES TREATED AT MALVERN,
AND A
PROSPECTUS OF THE WATER CURE ESTABLISHMENT
AT THAT PLACE.

BY
JAMES WILSON, M.D.,
PHYSICIAN TO HIS SERENE HIGHNESS PRINCE NASSAU, MEMBER
OF THE ROYAL COLLEGE OF SURGEONS, LONDON, &c. &c.
AND
JAMES M. GULLY, M.D.
FELLOW OF THE ROYAL PHYSICAL SOCIETY, EDINBURGH, OF THE
ROYAL MEDICO-CHIRURGICAL SOCIETY, LONDON, &c. &c.

The popular Dr Gully, 1808-1883.   *The doctors' Water-Cure book, 1843.*   *The pioneer, Dr Wilson, 1807-1867.*

pond in South Field not far from the Priory Church, the word 'Hay' originally meaning a forest clearing for animals, but the well is now hidden underground behind the Baptist Church. From these small beginnings, only four years later the successful Dr Wilson could begin to build his impressive new "Hydropathic Establishment" opposite the Hay Well, now Park View, at a cost of £18,000. It housed seventy or eighty patients and was called the *"Hydropathic Palace"* by some. *"The system of baths is complete, embracing warm, tepid, and cold Spray, Douche, Shower,*

The "Hydropathic Establishment" with the garden bath-houses on right, c1855.

COMING TO MALVERN.

WHAT I AM ABLE TO DO ON LEAVING.

Needle and Shallow Baths, on the principal floors, both for local and general application; while in the Bath-houses adjoining the establishment, are to be found Wave, Flowing-Sitz, Hot-air, Russian, Vapour, and every description of modern hydropathic baths and processes." Here an anonymous *"Moist Visitor"*, the sharp and satirical writer Joseph Leech, who was actually the editor of the Bristol Times, found a circle of patients around the Hay Well, *"All at work filling themselves like so many water casks."* At St Ann's Well he reported *"by this time they had, I suspect, swallowed enough, if well shaken, to make them rattle"* and at the old Ditchford Well by the turnpike on Ledbury Road he *"found another group of aquatic pilgrims blowing themselves out"*.

A DRINK AT ST ANNE'S WELL.

A drink at the Willow Spring.

The stressed and worn out Joseph Leech had come to Malvern to recuperate and was taking the water cure as a patient of Dr Wilson. *"After a short walk to warm myself, I hired a donkey to make the ascent. The donkeys form fully half the regular population of Malvern, and from their social and statistical importance I shall probably take occasion to confer a notice upon them."*

Donkeys on Victoria Drive, the zig-zag road up to St Ann's Well, c1890.

Rare stereoscope of St Ann's Well cottage with donkey-woman and riders c1845.

When he arrived Leech had the stated intention of ridiculing the water cure, but notes from his diary reveal that in fact he felt he had benefited from the treatments, particularly the frightening 'Douche Bath'. *"The man pulled the string – a momentary rush, like a*

THE CRUEL DOUCHE.

SEE HOW I AM TREATED.

thunderstorm, was heard above me, and the next second the water came roaring through the pipe like a lion upon its prey, and struck me on the shoulders with a merciless bang, spinning me like a teetotem. … For a minute and a half I remained under this water-spout, buffeting fiercely, until the cold column had cudgelled me as hot as a coal – aye, black and blue too; but, good gracious, what a glorious luxury – a nervous but still ecstatic luxury, that made you cry out at once in terror and rapture." Soon afterwards he declared to Dr Wilson that this was *"the primest luxury of all … It stimulates, it invigorates, it warms, and gives you for the time the vitality of a thousand men"*.

Cartoon of Joseph Leech riding his mule to a remote corner of the hills to smoke a surreptitious cigar. Illustration from "Three Weeks in Wet Sheets", 1851.

Diet and exercise were strictly controlled when taking the water cure and though obedient to most of Dr Wilson's dictates, Leech confessed to being guilty of surreptitiously breaking one of his laws. *"I hired a mule, and to be as far as possible out of reach of the danger of discovery, started for a remote and unfrequented spot in the hills between the Beacon and the Sugar-loaf. Having reached my destination, I dismissed the boy and mule, the former with a gratuity and a guilty look. … I waited till both were out of sight then looked around to ascertain that there was no one like Dr Wilson in view, and having satisfied myself that there was no cause for fear*

– that the coast was clear, I pulled out the cigar case and light. … Oh, the delicious, soothing comfort of those first few whiffs after a week's abstinence!" (Three Weeks in Wet Sheets, by a Moist Visitor, 1851)

"Lively Donkeys". Etching published by Rock & Co., 1855.

Five years after this humorous publication, Cuthbert Bede continued in a similar vein. *"If we were statistically called upon to arrange the natural productions of Malvern into three great heads, we would select for the three divisions – donkeys, mule-chairs, and round hats; with subdivisions into great and little donkeys, stubborn and tractable donkeys, shying and kicking donkeys, donkeys that go forwards, donkeys that go backwards, donkeys that are impervious to pins, donkeys that are callous to sticks, donkeys wot would, and donkeys wot wouldn't go."*

Donkey-chair waiting for hire at the Priory Gateway, c1860.

The *"mule-chairs"* or cars were a form of small carriage for two and were apparently unique to Malvern. *"A donkey-carriage to hold one costs two shillings for the ascent; a chair to hold two, four shillings; and a mule or pony carriage in which three people may ride, costs five shillings."* Whilst women controlled the donkey stands, *"The men attend to the mule-cars and to the riding mules, which latter are usually bestridden by the male visitors"*. Joseph Leech and a lawyer friend took a ride in one 'car' to Little Malvern church; *"We made the journey in a mule car - a pleasant, light, whisking little vehicle, ingenious to the place. The afternoon was fine and the driver communicative"*. On nearing their destination, *"our driver advised us to dismount and walk through the gate to avoid the toll. … As we expected, the man at the gate demanded sixpence"*. After the exchange of some mischievous legal banter it seems that they had *"had more than sixpence worth of fright or fun out of him, paid the toll and passed on"*.

After drinking the Waters.

Satirical writing had been very much in vogue since at least the beginning of the century and as well as the water-curists, fun was also made of the change of headgear necessary when elegant tourists took to breezy rides on the donkeys and mule-chairs. To replace their inappropriate top hats and elaborate bonnets "round hats" of all kinds were worn by the gentry, including straw boating hats and rugby caps, plus soft felt hats for ladies. The ridiculing of the patients and the donkey riders had became the subject of a series of popular etchings published not only by Lamb, but mainly by Rock and Co. in 1855, both singly, in books, on china souvenirs and by the end of the century as postcards. These light-hearted sketches were sold in the town's souvenir shops and at St Ann's Well as harmless fun, although today both these literary and artistic caricatures are regarded by some as having seriously contributed to the demise of the water cure.

An Air Douche, on the summit of the Beacon.

However, until the 1920s Ward Lock's popular Malvern guide continued to assure people that *"Many visitors make use of the donkeys that stand for hire at rates fixed by the Urban District Council. … Even invalids can ascend the 'breezy mountain sides', and they need not stop short of the highest summit, for nine miles of smooth, firm roads enable the ascent to be made in carriages drawn by ponies and donkeys. Numerous also are the saddle-donkeys that from Malvern's earliest days as a health resort have afforded a popular mode of progression up the hills"*.

The famous donkeys continued to be the subject of images promoting Malvern and St Ann's Well, now on humorous postcards c1910. The first postcards were produced in 1894.

A 'Lucky Heather' fairing and three crested china donkeys sold as popular souvenirs in Malvern's shops during the 19th century.

Malvern

Bloomfield

Boast Malvern that thy springs revive
The drooping patient scarce alive;
Where as he gathers strength to toil
Not e'en thy heights his spirits foil,
But nerve him on to bless, t'inhale
and triumph in the morning gale;
Or noon's transcendant glories give
the vig'rous touch that bids him live.
Perhaps e'en now he stops to breathe,
Surveying the expanse beneath;
Now climbs again where keen winds blow,
And holding his beaver to his brow;
skims o'er Worc'ster's spires away,
Where sprung the blush of rising day.

8 - Living for Donkeys' Years

Donkeys live longer than horses or ponies - 40 years was not unusual then or today. Throughout the 19th century not only was the longevity of the donkeys remarked upon, but at a time when life expectancy for the working classes was only 35 to 40 years, the

Woodcut by Mabel Varley, postcard c1930.

long lives of those Malvern residents who had always drunk spring water also became a focus of attention. There was a popular old proverb, *"If he dwells around the Malvern Hill, a man may live as long as he wille".*

The Clifton family lived in St Ann's Well from 1815 when the cottage was built, renting it for five guineas a year from the Foley Estate. Married in 1794, Hester, *"a very upright and correct lady"*, and her husband John supplied water cure visitors with refreshments in the terraced *"Tea Gardens"*.   Each morning they had to carry their daily supplies up the steep hill on donkeys and several

Early picture of donkeys at St Ann's Well with the bath-house on the left.   Previous page - *Donkey riders on Foley Terrace, c1840.*

early illustrations show donkeys and riders near the well entrance and climbing the hills behind. From 1820 the family also provided hot and cold bath treatments in a nearby small building, also shown in some contemporary etchings. In their first year at the well their unmarried daughter Mary, aged twenty, gave birth to a son who only lived until he was thirty. Hester died in 1826, but John lived on for a further twenty years, his long life attributed to the pure water, clear air and exercise. Mary then became head of the household and ran the business, helped by her niece and a servant Elizabeth Drinkwater, until about 1860 when the octagon was built. It was claimed that John was 91 when he died in 1846, although *"the Registrar would not believe he was so old, but eventually conceded an age of ninety on the Death Certificate"*. *(Paul Clifton, 2005)*

In 1834 Dr Addison *"computed that in the parishes on the eastern side of the Malvern Hills there were then living, at eighty years of age, nearly double the number in all England; and at ninety, three times the number, without taking into account still older persons."* Lord Bacon reported a Morris dance of eight men in the parish of Cradley on the western side of the hills *"whose years put together made up to 800; that which was*

An ageing Malvern donkey-woman and donkey boy, hand-coloured etching c1840.

Busy donkey scene at St Ann's Well with the new octagon, 1875.

77

Donkeys and visitors at St Ann's Well, 1910.

Tired basket seller sitting at the top of the Beacon, c1890.

"View from the Beacon looking West", 1877.

wanting of a hundred in some, super-abounding in others." While *"In January 1835, at Great Malvern, there were sixty persons residing, who were 70 years and upwards."* (Notes and Queries for Worcestershire, John Noake 1856) In the British Medical Journal of November 23rd 1872 Dr Grindrod claimed that Malvern had the lowest mortality rate of any watering place in England.

From the 1830s Lucy Dalton regularly transported ginger beer and cakes along difficult country paths from Mathon to West Malvern to sell to visitors, dying in 1884 aged 95. Donkey woman Mrs Steed lived in a little cottage on the West Malvern hillside near the public springs and for many years hired out donkeys, which *"patiently took old and young to the top of the Beacon."* Born in 1811, long before the height of the commercial water cure, *"She lived to be 97, and to within a week of her death, she was able to go about alone, keep her house in order, and dig her garden. In the cottage she brought up eleven children. After her death in 1908 the charming little thatched cottage was pulled down."* (*The West Malvern Book, W.I. & Mrs E. Knight, 2000*)

In the 1850s, as well as donkey stands at several springs in West Malvern, the village now

Mrs Mary Bannister, born 1824, in the centre of three elderly donkey-women resting, c1885.

Mrs Anna Maria Layland, born 1820, with her donkey-chair for hire in the 1890s.

Mr Dobbs with his dog and donkey cart, Westminster Bank, stereoscope, c1850.

also contained a number of water cure facilities. The hydropath Dr Charles Grindrod could be regularly consulted by his patients, including a Mrs Wordsworth, at 'West Villas' in West Malvern Road and journeys to and from here were often made by riding over the ridge from Great Malvern on hill donkeys and in donkey carts and chairs. In 1997 local resident Vera Jones, who died in 2008 aged over 80, told me that the pair of tiny Victorian gothic cottages at the entrance to nearby Ebrington Road, now called 'Roseneath', were built to treat the male and female hydropathy patients separately. The left cottage was solely for gentlemen's use and the right for ladies. The cottages were originally called St James' Baths and had 'demoiselle' or Danzell Spring water piped directly to them from the hill just above. Vera remembered that each had a large drain in the centre of the small ground floor room to take away the quantities of water during treatments, so these may have included the infamous cold 'Douche' of the water-cure.

St James' Baths now Roseneath Cottages, built for water-cure treatments in the 19th century.

Former St James' public Well House, 2008.

On the other side of the road was a well house for public use, also supplied from the Danzell Spring and this building was later incorporated into the terrace as the rear section of the present Village Hall. In the early 20th century old Mr Gardiner set out from North Malvern, calling here each morning with his horse and cart on his journey to Wyche Cutting and back to the Clock Tower. He was employed by the Council to keep the street and grass verges along this route clean and to pick up any debris such as animal droppings and tree branches onto his cart. When he reached Ebrington Road he would turn on the stopcock in the road junction, which controlled the Danzell Spring supply to the well rooms. Deaths of elderly residents in 1909 in West Malvern included Mrs Saunders aged 104 and Mr King aged 102, and again their longevity was attributed to good spring water, clean air and regular exercise on the hills.

The restored Royal Malvern Well spout today.

At Wyche Cutting a donkey stand used to exist in the grounds of 'Ryland Cottage' on Beacon Road, behind the once popular tourist spot of the Royal Malvern Well Spa and the stable building was still in existence until the 1990s. William Ryland, the Mayor of Bewdley, had built the Royal Malvern Well spout in 1870 and donkeys were used to carry visitors up to the well and later spa from Great Malvern, probably via the Beacon and St Ann's Well, and through Wyche Cutting to and from Malvern Wells. He provided this public spout in gratitude for his recovery from consumption after regularly drinking the spring water here, which came originally from the holy well of St Thomas still in a cottage close beside the site.

After building the public spout, the gentry appealed to Ryland to create a well room for their own use. He then went on to build the Royal Malvern Well Spa, an ambitious domed hall seating 2000 people, *"opened in May 1883 by Jenny Lind* (the famous singer)*, in the greatest grandeur, before a gathering of all the Worcestershire and Herefordshire elite."* *(Worcestershire Archaeology & Local History Newsletter, 1979)* This included a *"Spa Pump Room"*, a refreshment bar, a suite of water cure baths for *"tourists and invalids"* and an art gallery. A medallion was struck to celebrate its opening which bore the words,

*"From pole to pole let the fame be
    unfurled
of the marvellous water, the best in the
    world
for every known ailment, as thousands
    can tell
who have drank and were cured
    at the Royal Malvern Well."*

The medallion struck for the Spa opening in 1883.

But for most visitors the spa could only be reached by equine transport and two years later the attractive and more easily accessible Assembly Rooms in Great Malvern were opened, now Malvern Theatres, and the Royal Spa became known as 'Ryland's Folly', closing down in 1895. Ryland was bankrupted and the site was soon vandalised and became derelict. It was demolished in 1937, but the original Royal Malvern Well public spout remains and still has a good flow of water. However, old Mr Thomas Jenkins who had sold his cottage and spring to Ryland in the 1860s for the building of the well, lived to the ripe old age of 107, dying in 1909.

The Royal Malvern Well Spa building in about 1890.

"The Assembly Rooms and Pleasure Gardens", Great Malvern, 1885.

The Royal Malvern Spa

(Anonymous)

Now I saw a great crowd had surrounded the spring,
Such as might from its curative fame be expected;
Some on crutches, some each arm in a sling,
And others had bladders or kidneys infected'
Aye! all looked most miserably sad and dejected.
Lo! they drank of the nerve-bracing water designed
By Nature to strengthen both body and mind,
And rejoicing they left their disorders behind.

(Extract from a long poem published in 1883)

9 - Poverty and the Donkey Drivers

Coming originally from the scrubby terrain on the fringe lands of African and Asian deserts, donkeys could survive on a sparser diet than ponies and horses and so were cheaper to keep as a means of transport. Donkeys were also used as dairy animals by the poor, both to provide themselves with milk and to sell to the gentry *"as a wash for the complexion"* in the manner of Cleopatra. *"Malvern visitors who need asses' milk can readily procure it, if they make their wishes known at the confectioners, or to the old lady at the Abbey Gateway, who now in her eighty-sixth year presides over game and green-grocery, and still announces herself as 'sausage-maker to her Royal Highness the Duchess of Kent'."* (*Malvern Donkeys, Cuthbert Bede, 1862*)

Donkeys were now popular and reliable beasts of burden for the poor in villages, towns and cities across Britain, particularly in London, the home of many of Malvern's

Mrs E. Clay presides over her stall at the Priory Gateway selling game animals and birds, groceries and asses milk, c1850. Courtesy Malvern Library.

aristocratic visitors. But Cuthbert Bede was critical of the care they received in the capital. *"Any beast that is well fed and humanely treated, will in the end be cheaper, become more serviceable, than one that is half starved and brutally beaten; and it could be wished that costermongers would take this low view of the case, if they are not able to take a higher one."* In 1893 the prolific ownership of donkeys by the poor in East London was written about by W. J. Gordon, who noted that there were then over 2000 donkey deliveries a day to the markets of Covent Garden alone. He described how the poorest costermongers in Covent Garden would develop a business by firstly selling goods from a basket, then *"from that he advances to a hand-truck; and from that, when he has amassed sufficient capital, he rises to the dignity of the donkey-cart"*.

But donkeys also carried the social stigma of poverty, making it unacceptable for the city elite to ride on them when at home, yet after Princess Victoria's visit to Malvern, riding on the hire-donkeys here had become a novel attraction for the gentry. Joseph Leech observed *"In Malvern every body may be seen beside or astride an ass; the consequence is you have no false shame about taking an outside place on one of the patient animals to whatever point you please to go. A small fortune would hardly tempt me to ride so mounted by the Commercial Rooms of Bristol, under a flanking fire of jokes from my friends. In Malvern, however, when Peers and Members of Parliament passed you thus humbly accommodated, you feel no hesitation in following their example, since such was the fashion"*.

Rare early photo of a Malvern donkey stand with impoverished women and donkey-boys c1850.

A woman and her hire-donkeys at a stand with her young children waiting under a gas lamp at dawn or dusk. Watercolour by Mary Brandling, 1856. Courtesy Malvern Library.

Although in the Malverns impoverished women usually owned and ran the fleets of hire-donkeys from the stands at the village spouts, hill springs, or in the town, it was always small children who acted as drivers, leading the donkeys and climbing with them on their steep hill walks carrying visitors. They worked from dawn until dusk and when riders were going too fast the young donkey-drivers tried to slow them down to prevent accidents. But the gentry were

Young drivers with their donkey-hire team on a hill path, c1890

apparently oblivious to the dangers as well as to the exhaustion of their child-drivers and steeds, and only saw going at speed as great fun. *"The driver had hold of the mule's tail, either to steer him in the right way, or to aid his own progress. The rider was looking as if he thoroughly enjoyed these Malvern recreations. The sheep browsing amid the fern, gorse, and foxgloves, looked up as he clattered past, with something of*

Donkey-boy trying to slow down Dr Birch who was racing his mount. By Cuthbert Bede, 1861. Courtesy of Database of Mid-Victorian Wood-Engraved Illustration, Cardiff University.

Humorous postcard c1915.

MAKING A BARGAIN FOR DONKEYS.

Small children riding a donkey with panniers, photo by Francis Earl, c1880.

astonishment." Cuthbert Bede recorded that after a busy day one boy-driver complained *"We was at it from morning till night, and they all on 'em wanted to canter. One chap clapped a pair o' spurs on, and wouldn't take 'em off, though I told him I should tell the perlice. It was as much as I could do to keep up"*.

Bede also observed how the children of the gentry were catered for; *"Donkeys are provided with panniers for those little trots who cannot be trusted to hold onto the pommels; and for these double-barrelled donkeys double price is charged. Malvern is a famous place for children, and they could not be brought to few healthier spots for their rambles, scrambles, gambols and donkey-rides"*. But this was in stark contrast to the lives of the child-drivers, who climbed the hills up to ten times a day, were *"not allowed to mount the donkeys on their return journey"* and were paid very little if anything at all. Often they had to stand, watch and wait while their middle-class clients enjoyed eating their picnics and admiring the views.

"When the rider pays for his steed, the driver always asks for a gratuity for himself; and, as his request is usually complied with, the more journeys he makes, the more coppers he receives. The donkey-proprietors do not pay the boys in money, but in lodgings and food." (*Leisure Hour, Malvern Donkeys, Cuthbert Bede, 1862*) At that time the charge for climbing the hill was nine pence for donkeys, though a shilling

was usually demanded, and eighteen pence for a mule but less was often taken, with the descent costing half price if their client did not want to walk down. Even at the beginning of the 20th century the donkeys could still be hired for nine pence an hour and six pence for every subsequent hour, or 3s 6d for the whole day, but the donkey-children only received about two shillings a week for this work.

A hillside picnic with champagne watched by the impoverished
donkey-boys waiting with their mounts, c1850.

Mistreatment of the donkeys by their young drivers was sometimes reported. *"A worthy gentleman was called 'the donkey's friend', because he laboriously endeavoured to instil principles of humanity into the hearts of the young donkey-drivers. …The Malvern donkeys are certainly thwacked more than is needful, and I am not without my suspicions of pins being somewhat too freely used in connection with the extremities of the donkey and the driver's stick; but saving these facts and suspicions, I am glad to say that the donkeys are well cared for to enable them to endure the hard work of the season. …Thus they are not stinted on their food and the mediation of their tender-hearted riders can save them from gratuitous thwacks if not from surreptitious pins"* (Leisure Hour, Cuthbert Bede, 1862)

When Joseph Leech first arrived he observed, *"The donkey-boys returning with their beasts invariably as they pass bestow on the traveller's animal upward bound a vigorous whack, so that by these occasional contributions, and what you can do yourself in the shape of thrashing, you contrive to move on. At first I felt disposed to resent the donation as impertinence, by bestowing a similar stripe on the shoulders of the youthful donor, but I soon discovered it was the custom of the place, and meant as a kindness."*

The cruelty to animals in both war and commerce had become a great national concern, and the Malvern Society for the Prevention of Cruelty to Animals was founded in 1865 to try to stem the local abuse. They installed a number of animal troughs in the district, including a spring water trough at the entrance to Great Malvern Station in 1881, for watering the horses, ponies, mules and donkeys whilst they were waiting to pick up passengers taking excursions around the hills. This little trough still exists beside the main entrance, now usually filled with plants. In the 1990s the RSPCA opposed moves to re-establish donkeys at St Ann's Well, although they are still used on the steep slopes of Clovelly in Devon and have just been reintroduced to carry shopping in panniers uphill at Chalford in Gloucestershire.

'The Orphans of Malvern' was a popular book of typically Victorian moral tales originally published in the1840s and again in 1874. One story tells of poverty-stricken local orphan called Mary befriending a sick girl who is visiting Great Malvern to improve her health. The child's parents reward Mary's kindness by giving her a donkey, which she could then hire out to earn a living and so escape the Workhouse in Worcester Road near Link Top. In real life Chambers recorded in 1817, *"So crowded was Malvern one season, that a lady of rank and fashion, with her equipage and servants, were actually obliged to be sent to the Workhouse. It is now the custom, during the season, to let out this house to visitors,*

The orphan Mary leads her sick friend uphill on a donkey, 1845.

92

Disgruntled donkey-boys with sticks wait for hire on the Beacon, 1900.

Donkey-children on a hill path.

The small MSPCA animal trough installed in 1881 at Great Malvern Station.

and the money gained in this way is applied to the funds for maintaining the poor."

The benevolent Dr Grindrod of water cure fame helped the poor and illiterate donkey boys by founding a small school for them in the 1850s at the foot of the Worcestershire Beacon. Here they were taught the rudiments of 'the three R's' but it was closed in 1870 when compulsory primary education came in. At the beginning of the century Lady Lyttelton had begun a Sunday School for poor children above the Unicorn, the public house still in existence today. John Chambers writes in 1817 that she *"continues to watch over the morals of the lower orders of society round Malvern, in the welfare of which place she has always felt much interested."*

Donkey-girl at the Toposcope, 1900.

Another now familiar benefactor, Charles Morris, built the North Malvern National School for local children opposite his 'Tank' spout in 1838. The Tank tower still bears a plaque asking the poor to pray for the blessing of Morris.

"YE YOUNG AND AGED POOR
PRAY
THAT THE BLESSINGS OF GOD
BE ABUNDANTLY POURED UPON HIM
WHO HAS HERE POURED
ABUNDANT BLESSINGS UPON YOU."

In April 1876 the West Malvern village school recorded a request from Mr Watson to one donkey-hire family, asking that their child Arthur Price, who was frequently on the hill donkey driving, should be allowed to attend school more regularly as *"he is a good sharp boy and I regret him being away so much."* However the records show that the boy's name had to be removed from the register in March 1888, *"As his mother can't spare him any longer at school."* (*West Malvern, Valerie Goodbury, 1994*) By the 1880s numbers of schoolboys from the village school would regularly become donkey drivers during the summer holidays.

A donkey-driver waits as young 'toffs' admire the views and pose for photos, 1910.

A young 'toff' in a boater is photographed while the tired driver sits in the bracken.

It seems that the young donkey drivers suffered some abuse and ridicule from visitors, if not blows. There evidently was some sympathy among the townsfolk for the impoverished donkey boys and girls who often became the butt of jokes and insults. *"The donkeys and horses of our watering places are often a hard used and much abused race, and generally the fault lies with those who use them, and not in those to whose care they are committed. The party who engages an animal has it in his power to prevent an undue strain on its energies, as well as the improper application of the whip. Donkey drivers are not infrequently made impudent or presuming by undue familiarity, or by being converted into* objects of merriment and joke." (*Anonymous quote in Malvern Country by Vincent Waite 1968*) But by the turn of the century not only the middle-class riders but particularly the young 'Toffs' with their straw boaters, had themselves become objects of ridicule.

Donkey of Brown

Patricia Higgins

Donkey of brown please let me know
Why is it that you go so slow?
He turned round gently to me and said
I have some sense in my little brown head.
By hurrying so as you go by
You miss the beauty in earth and sky.
So I took his advice and looked around,
And saw diamonds in dew drops on the ground.
Daises that dance in the sun's golden ray,
Things I missed as I hurried each day.
Gold in the buttercups, clouds in the blue,
What the donkey said was perfectly true.

(Courtesy of the Sathya Sai Sanctuary)

As well as the numerous hire-donkeys bringing visitors to the summit of the Worcestershire Beacon, for more than forty years local women had been carrying baskets of food and goods to the top to sell to tourists. Seeing a commercial opportunity here John V. Down, a professional photographer who took many of Malvern's early photos, erected stone built refreshment shops on the Beacon summit at considerable expense in about 1873. The buildings also housed a 'camera obscura' to attract the gentry indoors. This invention projected a live 360-degree panorama of the surrounding landscape on a table inside the building. Down had previously run a successful

photographic studio beside the old bath-house at St Ann's Well since 1855. But his new development on the Beacon evidently created tensions with the impoverished outdoor sales women. In 1875 Down was prosecuted and fined for attacking a seventy-year old woman from Colwall, who had been selling goods from baskets on the hill top.

John Down's photographic studio beside the bath-house at St Ann's Well, c1860. Photography was invented in the 1820s and cameras first became generally available in Britain from 1840.

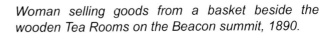

Woman selling goods from a basket beside the wooden Tea Rooms on the Beacon summit, 1890.

Stone refreshment buildings on the Beacon summit and on the left the camera-obscura building with its rotating mirror on the roof, c1875.

Elegant visitors to the camera-obscura on St Ann's Delight with John Down in the centre, c1865.

A donkey-woman holds her animal as a family is photographed with their young baby, by John Down c1870.

He had originally leased the site from the landowner John Hornyold, who made him demolish the premises in 1878. Down used the reclaimed stone to build 'the Observatory' in West Malvern, now 'the Broomhill'.

The Malvern Hills Conservators were founded in 1884 and then approved the building of a wooden refreshment hut on the same site at the top of the Beacon. From 1889 at the age of fifty-four until her death aged 76, Mrs Elizabeth Price of West Malvern ran a successful tearoom in these large huts with the help of her two donkeys which carried up the daily supplies in wicker panniers. Donkeys were still being used for this work in the 1930s. *"As we neared the top of the Worcestershire Beacon once more we were in the clouds. A ghostly procession of donkeys suddenly appeared, their panniers heavily laden with provisions for the refreshment hut."* (*Malvern Gazette, October 1931*)   The

café was always a very popular spot for visitors to pause for a cup of tea and admire the long distant views, over at least fourteen counties on a clear day, from the 'Toposcope' or 'Indicator' erected in 1897. At numerous stands below, donkeys and drivers were readily available to take visitors up to this spot.

Mrs Elizabeth Price proprietor of the new wooden 'Tea-Rooms', c1895.

Sam, Elizabeth and Rene Price taking water and goods in procession up to the Tea-Rooms, c1900.

Donkeys for hire outside the wooden Tea Rooms with the camera obscura apparently still in place.

Donkeys for hire on top of the Beacon. Watercolour by A.R. Quinton, c1912.

Valerie Goodbury's valuable research recorded that every morning Mrs Price would climb to the hut on the hill summit with the donkeys, returning at dusk. *"One donkey carried assorted necessities, the other, two copper containers full of water obtained from the spring at the top of Westminster Bank."* (*West Malvern, Valerie Goodbury, 1994*) Her son Sam and his wife Rene then ran the business with three donkeys until 1932, when their niece Miss Irene Taylor took over. The donkeys were allowed to stay on the hill throughout the working day, sometimes tethered to a slip rope between two iron rings that can still be found on the rocky summit. After the Second World War the hut was called 'The Beacon Café' but sadly it burnt down in late January 1989 and despite much local support, four years later the House of Lords refused permission for the Conservators to have it rebuilt.

Detail of "A Fair Field Full of Folk", the surviving one of a pair of large oil paintings by Alys Woodman c1950, that was removed from the Beacon Café for restoration a week before it burnt down, and is now in the Hills Conservators' offices.

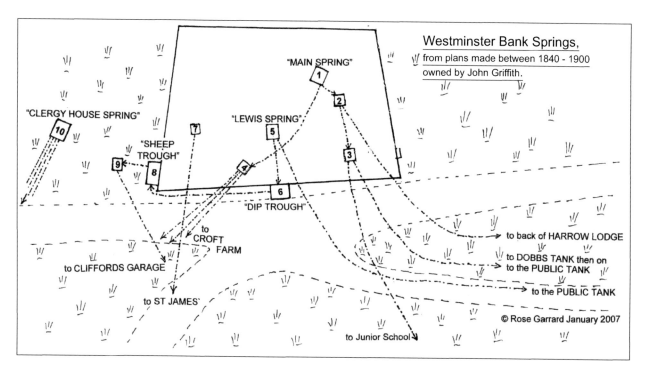

Westminster Bank Springs,
from plans made between 1840 - 1900
owned by John Griffith.

"MAIN SPRING"

"CLERGY HOUSE SPRING"

"LEWIS SPRING"

"SHEEP TROUGH"

"DIP TROUGH"

to CROFT FARM

to CLIFFORDS GARAGE

to ST JAMES'

to Junior School

to back of HARROW LODGE

to DOBBS TANK then on to the PUBLIC TANK

to the PUBLIC TANK

© Rose Garrard January 2007

Plans made between 1840 and 1900 show that there were at least three springs in a tight cluster at Westminster Bank as well as a public spout, a 'sheep trough' and a 'dip trough', making it an ideal place for watering donkeys. The springs supplied a third of the village and were once owned by Westminster Abbey who were given the manor of Mathon in 1546 by Henry VIII, including the land that later became West Malvern. In the 19th century the 'Lewis Spring' supplied the Westminster Bank spout, the Morris public spout in West Malvern Road, as well as the Vicarage. The 'St James' source supplied the main house, cottages, water-gardens and estate of Lady Howard De Walden. The 'Clergy House Spring' supplied several private houses named after saints, plus the St Edward's Orphanage for boys, where it was rumoured in the village that 'fallen women' quietly came to have their babies. The 'Main Spring' was piped from the source down to Croft Farm in the valley below.

Dip Trough at Westminster Bank Springs.

Rosebud Cottage, 2008.

Equine transport near the Westminster Arms Hotel.

From 1853 at the age of eighteen, thirty-six years before she took over the refreshment hut, Mrs Elizabeth Price and her husband lived in Rosebud Cottage at the bottom of the steep slope to Westminster Bank Springs. She stabled her donkeys beside the cottage and in her younger years may have hired these out to go up to the Beacon from the Westminster upper springs or from a lower stand at the new Morris Tank and public spout in the main road. The cottage was flanked on the southern corner by the Westminster Arms Hotel, which would have attracted plenty of well-to-do customers to a donkey station nearby. Earlier in the 1840s John Jones the blacksmith had lived and worked at Rosebud Cottage and during the 1980s Mr Turner who lived at 'St Francis', found many donkey shoes in his garden next door.

The boisterous behaviour of the donkey boys, particularly on Sundays, was often complained about to the Hills Conservators. It seems that rather than attend school, they would run wild with their donkeys, racing their steeds on the hills or bathing and splashing in the spring pool

Donkey-children waiting for hire on the hill ridge, c1910.

at Hay Slad, causing much annoyance to visitors. One complaint from Mr Salmon, probably of the Royal Well Mineral Water Company, was reported in the Malvern Advertiser in 1876. *"Upon the nuisance caused at Hay Slad by the boys who fetch water with donkey carts – By the present arrangement the barrels have to be filled with buckets and the boys consequently have to be loitering about a long time and thus become a nuisance to the visitors passing that spot – Mr Salmon suggests that something should be done whereby the barrels could be placed immediately under the spout so as to fill quickly."*

In 1886 the natural pool was drained, with little effect, as two years later there were still complaints about the boys misbehaving by dipping themselves into the source itself when collecting water by donkey-cart, as well as swearing and being cruel to their animals. In 1893 the present Malvern stone trough and spout were installed for *"the*

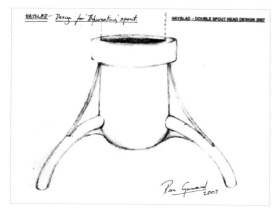

Above: Hay Slad spout today with new bifurcating spout suggested by David Armitage (AONB).
Left: Design for new spout by Rose Garrard, 2007.

benefit of man and animals" but the site was regularly vandalised for a number of years, though this was thought not to be the donkey boys doing, but the acts of some disgruntled inhabitants living below in Mathon village, concerned that their water supply had been tampered with.

But the misdemeanours of the donkey boys did not go unpunished. The stocks and whipping post in North Malvern Road are the remaining evidence of a feudal form of punishment metered out to both adults and children who caused trouble. The sentences included whipping, fines and ridicule, plus flogging for graver offences. In Victorian Malvern *"A single Magistrate settled the quarrels of the market-women, who, not being able to read or write, did all their business by memory or tallies. He had the Donkey-boys whipped when necessary, sent thieves to prison, and ruffians to the Assizes where they were often sentenced to be hanged."* (*A Little City Set on a Hill, C.F. Severn Burrow, 1948*)

Stocks and whipping post in North Malvern Road, 1930.

Victorian illustration of the use of stocks and a whipping post, showing two young boys being dragged to be whipped for scrumping apples, held tightly by a magistrate.

Evening

"A lady", 1801

Where Malvern rears her sky-capped head,
 and smiling health has fixed her court;
Where purest streams their blessings shed
 and balmy zephyrs laughing sport,
I often wander forth at eve
 to view the soft retreat of day;
The tranquil shades my mind relieve
 as night unfolds her cloak of grey,
Where then no footsteps mark the hill,
 or sounds obtrusive strike the ear,
I hear the low murmer of the rill
 that fills Hygea's fountains near.

(First published in "A Guide to the Watering Places for 1810")

11 - Droughts, Dangers and Celebrations

In 1865 over a quarter of Great Malvern's new buildings were lodging houses using large quantities of water and John Noake wrote *"During the last thirty or forty years Malvern has been rapidly growing as a place of resort, and is now become a town by Act of Parliament. A striking proof of its progress is afforded in the fact that in 1841 there were only sixty-four inhabited houses in the village, while in 1861 there were 992. ... The wet sheet and the douche bath are now in active requisition all the year round, there being located here no fewer than ten hydropathic physicians (independent of the regular faculty), and six establishments, devoted to this moist treatment."* (Worcestershire Relics, John Noake, 1877)

Belle Vue Terrace with carriage-hire stands, 1890.   Previous page - *Quarryman's Bridge, c1900.*

Before the development of the motorcar and tarmacadum road surfacing, the 19th century Malvern roads were broad tracks of rough earth and granite chippings, soft and muddy in the rains and full of dust following periods of severe drought. The Great Western and other regular horse-drawn coaches called at the Unicorn Inn, and Lord Macaulay commented *"on every road round Malvern coaches and flys pass you every ten minutes, to say nothing of irregular vehicles."*

Although today it may be difficult to imagine the roads of the Malverns busy with horses, ponies and donkeys, by now their numbers were already numerous and increasing rapidly. *"Yes the donkeys! They are among the unalterable fixtures of the place. ... The only change they experience is that of increase of numbers.   Malvern and its donkeys are simultaneously developed. As in other articles of traffic, so in this, the demand creates and regulates the supply; and, if Malvern has any local trade that is peculiarly its own, it is in donkeys."* (*Malvern Donkeys, Cuthbert Bede, 1862*)

The very first railway branch-line from Worcester had been constructed to Malvern Link in 1853 and the station was completed in 1859, delivering further water cure passengers in relative comfort, but they still needed equine road transport to complete their journeys, including donkeys from the nearby stand on Link Common. To help cope with all this extra traffic, from 1854 the streets of Great Malvern were watered every night and morning in dry weather to try to improve their worn and dusty surfaces. As the town's population continued to grow the prolific spring water supplies that had attracted so many people here began to prove inadequate.   By 1855 the lack of rain, plus the now numerous hydropathic

Steam train arriving at Malvern Link station in about 1862.

JUST A LINE FROM MALVERN.

Collage of donkeys on Malvern Link common, postcard 1909. There was a donkey-hire stand on the common near the Link station.

establishments taking supplies from the springs, caused increased shortages of water for domestic and animal use throughout the Malverns.

But by 1866, as well as the movement of horse carriages, pony traps, mules and donkeys, the numerous new building works in the expanding town needed frequent deliveries of heavy stone by horse drawn cart from the hillside quarries, which made

The single-storey 'Tank' in front of the quarry in North Malvern Road, 1836. Etching dedicated to Charles Morris's mother by Henry Lamb. The Quarrymans' Bridge and waterfall can be seen in the background.

the roads extremely dusty. People complained of being quickly covered in dust whether walking in the streets or sitting at home, so visitors began to stay away. This had a very negative effect on bookings at the many local hotels and boarding houses and consequently on the donkey-hire trade.

In North Malvern George McCann, a builder who owned a brickworks in Malvern Link, had completed the original single storey water 'Tank', well room and public spout in 1836, commissioned by Charles Morris. The Tank was at first supplied from a waterfall channelled from North Valley Spring, falling from under the new bridge at the top of the cliff high above, creating a dramatic cascade, 'enchanting' hill paths and 'picturesque' views to attract visitors. Although elegant houses and a hotel soon sprang up nearby,

Rare photo of Quarryman's Bridge and waterfall behind the Tank, c1880, with North Malvern Spout built in 1835 on the right. Courtesy of Malvern Museum.

the adjacent quarries also expanded and by 1876 most of the waterfall had disappeared from view having been piped underground to a new and larger service reservoir higher up the hill. From 1854 until 1944 Mary Bannister, her daughter Eliza and then her granddaughter Alice, ran a donkey-hire business from beside the Tank building and

Joseph Bannister aged 11, a reluctant donkey-boy made to work in the school holidays, c1900.

there was a donkey stable close by at the top of Pump Street. But as the spout in the well room was for domestic use only, horses, ponies and hire-donkeys used to be watered at an animal trough in the main road a short distance away, beside the stocks and whipping post.   The stocks have been on the present site since 1870 but were formerly on the site of Trinity Church when the corner was open common land.   Behind them a stone-built stray animal enclosure or 'pound' can still be seen today. Fines for any stray animals were severe, up to one pound for each, plus charges for their keep while impounded, and if these were not paid within a few days the animals were sold off.   This system is thought to have continued until the end of the 19th century to control animals causing damage by straying onto the roads and private land.

Many houses now had piped spring water and the first domestic water meters began to be introduced in Malvern to charge more fairly for the amount used. But the free water supply at the public spouts and hillside springs was essential and still relied upon by the poorer inhabitants, including the donkey-hire families who often couldn't afford piped water. From 1871 *"the rent for the supply of water to all houses and premises of more*

View of the growing town from North Hill with donkeys returning from Happy Valley. Etching by Newman 1871.

Donkeys probably coming to collect water at the Tank well room. Etching of the short tower, 1855.

Donkey-chair parked against a boulder at the ivy covered Tank tower.

than £10 rateable value is not to exceed one shilling for every 1,000 gallons of water supplied. £10 and under, the price is not to exceed six pence per 1,000 gallons." *(Report by C. Judson, MHDC Surveyor and Water Engineer, 1953)* Penalties for non-payment were fast and severe. If accounts were not paid within seven days the Local Water Board could cut off the supply and after a further seven days notice, would remove all meters and pipe-work, forcing residents to use the public spouts.

As many ordinary people could not afford time-pieces, the single storey building that fronted the underground Tank in North Malvern was crowned with a short tower in 1843, also built by Morris, to support a single clock. This not only enabled nearby quarry workers to arrive on time, but also local residents now knew exactly when the rock blasting would happen twice a day. But the clock was said to be a bad timekeeper, probably because of the force of the blasts from the quarries behind. In 1901

The extended height of the Clock Tower from the back after 1901.

a further two storeys were added to support a new clock, paid for by the Urban Council, with four gas-lit clock faces and a flagpole to celebrate the accession of Edward VII to the throne. The building then became known as 'the Clock Tower' and some minor damage from the blasts can still be seen today on the minute markers of the front clock face, which was actually cracked in two.

Curved stone sections of arch near the site of the collapsed reservoir, 2006.

As demand for water increased the Local Water Board began to construct a larger service reservoir on the hill above the Tank in order to regulate the spring water, but in 1872 this attempt ended in disaster. During a severe storm a torrent of water from the valley above caused the unfinished reservoir to collapse, injuring several workmen, apparently because the mortar was not fully set and the design was faulty. The site was abandoned and a second reservoir, which is still in use, was built slightly higher up the hillside with a capacity of 738,000 gallons. Although elsewhere ponies and donkeys were sometimes used in quarries and for construction, no record can be found of their use for this work in the Malverns. Rather than donkeys, an innovative steam lift was installed to carry the building blocks and materials to the reservoir site and this used to run up the blue brick stairway that still exists just below. The little Quarrymans' Bridge and

Quarrymans' bridge 2006.

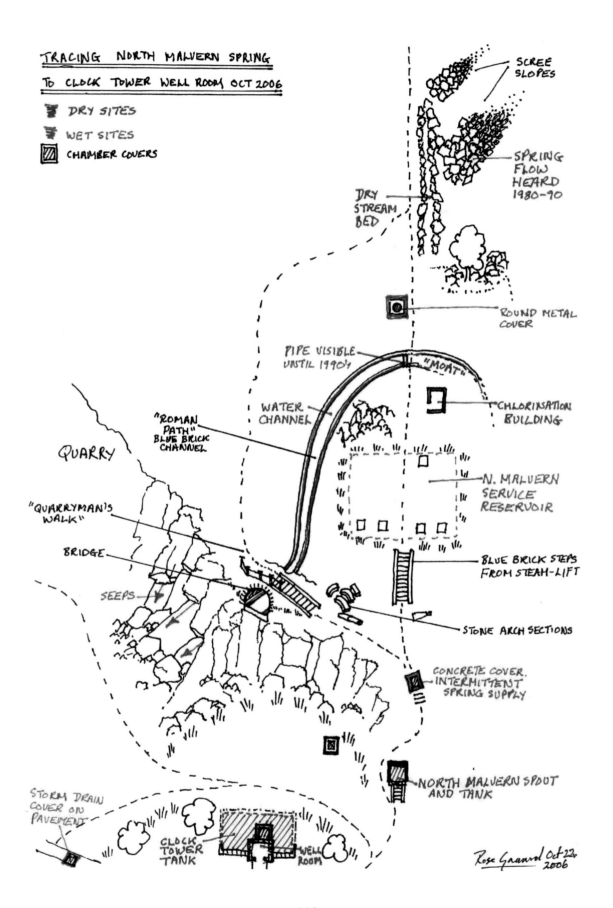

TRACING NORTH MALVERN SPRING
TO CLOCK TOWER WELL ROOM OCT 2006

DRY SITES
WET SITES
CHAMBER COVERS

SCREE SLOPES

SPRING FLOW HEARD 1980-90

DRY STREAM BED

ROUND METAL COVER

PIPE VISIBLE UNTIL 1990's

"MOAT"

CHLORINATION BUILDING

WATER CHANNEL

"ROMAN PATH" BLUE BRICK CHANNEL

QUARRY

N. MALVERN SERVICE RESERVOIR

"QUARRYMAN'S WALK"

BRIDGE

BLUE BRICK STEPS FROM STEAM-LIFT

SEEPS

STONE ARCH SECTIONS

CONCRETE COVER. INTERMITTENT SPRING SUPPLY

NORTH MALVERN SPOUT AND TANK

STORM DRAIN COVER ON PAVEMENT

CLOCK TOWER TANK

WELL ROOM

Rose Garrard Oct 22, 2006

118

substantial water channel, known originally as 'the Moat' or 'Roman Path', but now dry, can be still be found when climbing up the North Valley.

In March 1877 the local paper reported the use of the lift at the ceremonial *"public inspection"* of the huge empty arched structure of the new reservoir. *"The commanding escarpment of the hill, overlooking the North Malvern Post Office, was gay with bannerettes and streamers, with the sound of the harp and fiddle, the trumpet and the drum, the applause of men, and the merry voices of women and little ones. Immediately below the new reservoir there is a huge cairn of debris, and on an inclined plane immediately above this a steam lift has been in use, but on Monday this rather primitive looking machine underwent a transformation, … draped in pink and carpeted for the use of the ladies … so as to safely and comfortably transport about a dozen ladies at a time. From two o'clock until five it was incessantly*

The interior of the North Malvern Service Reservoir photographed when it was drained in the 1980s.

in requisition raising bevies of belles from the road to the mouth of the reservoir in the rocks, over a hundred feet above, and in bringing them down again. … Around the landing stage and the mouth of the reservoir there was a large concourse of people waiting their turn to descend inside. … The interior of the reservoir was reached by descending a cork-screw flight of good stone steps, which for the occasion were also provided with a stout temporary handrail, abundantly swathed in evergreens, which had the double effect of improving the appearance of this part of the structure, and hiding from the sight of the timorous the yawning gulf beneath them." (Malvern Advertiser, March 1877) But the reservoir proved to be too big to be completely filled from the intermittent spring source and eventually, in the early 20th century, treated water was pumped up to help fill it and to supplement the intermittent spring water to the public spout.

Ironically, the lack of spring water in the Malverns continued to be a huge problem for many years, particularly following the "Great Drought" of 1887 when little rain fell. Then the British Camp Reservoir, with a capacity of fifty million gallons, was built to supply the town from the hill springs above. It was opened by the Duchess of Teck in 1895 amidst great celebrations and when filled by heavy rainfall the following year it was heralded as the solution to all Great Malvern's water shortages. But as demand again increased it soon proved insufficient, the reservoir drying up completely during the drought of 1902. The following year water was piped here from boreholes at Bromsberrow. The building costs of the reservoir, to be paid by the relatively small community of Great Malvern, reached the huge sum of £60,000 raised by loans for the scheme, which were still being paid back by the inhabitants of the town in the 1950s.

The Clock Tower spout continued to supply free water to the local poor for many years and one family, who made a meagre living from taking in laundry, relied on this as their sole source until in 1947, when it and the animal trough were cut off to save water. The last practicing donkey-hire woman, Mrs Alice Betteridge who was the grand-daughter of Mary Bannister, worked her donkey team from here until a few years after the Second World War was declared in 1939. Her donkeys could be hired in the early morning from beside the Clock Tower to go to Great Malvern via Ivy Scar Rock and the hill path to Red Lion Bank, where they waited again for hire at the Happy Valley stand before going on up to the Beacon. In the 1940s heavy rocks blasted from the quarry killed one of Alice's donkey team, after which she gave up the hire business. (See final chapter)

Donkey riders on route to Happy Valley from North Hill, 1875.

North Malvern Quarry at the beginning of the 20th century, with the Clock Tower on the right.

The quarry explosions continued throughout the 1960s, frequently throwing dangerous showers of stones as far as Cowleigh Road onto the houses and people below. On one occasion in the early 20th century a large two hundred weight boulder was loosened by the shock and rolled downhill to the gate of Trinity Church Vicarage. *"Mr Thorpe brought two men with a wheelbarrow from the council's quarries and had the boulder conveyed to Page Bros' stores, where it turned the scale at the weight given. It was subsequently taken to the police station." (Malvern Memories, Malvern Gazette, Robert Hale, March 2008)* All quarrying on the hills finally ended in the 1970s following increasing protests from the Hills Conservators and both Hereford and Worcester County Councils. Malvern Town Council now owns the well room and Clock Tower itself, whilst the Conservators own the dry 50,000-gallon

Trinity Church and the Vicarage below the quarries, 1877.

The overgrown Clock Tower in 2005.

The new "Cascade Gates" installed in September 2007. Designed by Rose Garrard.

Work begins on uncovering the original brick path, October 2006.

underground water tank and its front supporting walls that flank the tower. In 1970 the spring water that had originally supplied the Tank and the well room spout was piped 'to waste' into the storm drain. In 2007 the direct but intermittent spring water supply to the spout was reconnected and the new forged iron 'Cascade Gates' that I designed in 2006, were made by the blacksmith Andrew Findlay at Eastnor and installed at the well room entrance. I had based the gate design on the curved forms of the hills and of flowing water, plus the ivy leaves that once covered the original Victorian short tower. The Malvern Hills Area of Outstanding Natural Beauty office in partnership with the Malvern Spa Association, the Town Council and the Malvern Hills Conservators had restored the building, the clock, the well room, the grounds and the spring water to the spout, with the help of a grant from the Heritage Lottery Fund.

The restored Clock Tower, 2008.

The Donkey

Thomas Hardy

Alas for the humble goal
That looms in life anon
Of a thoughtful Ass's foal
Like me, when I muse thereon!

Perhaps I shall pull a cart –
Perhaps I shall carry a pack –
Perhaps at a sea resort
I shall bear little boys on my back.

As well as the larger donkey teams it wasn't unusual for at least one person in a village to own a donkey or a mule and a cart, which they would hire out or lend to neighbours as transport. A journal kept by Sara Hutchinson, (a relative of the poet Wordsworth) recorded her summer walks with her invalid sister, often riding on a donkey hired from Betty Hardwick in West Malvern. On June 13th 1863 Sara wrote *"… bethought ourselves, we would go on to the Beacon, mounted Elizabeth on Betty's donkey, and set off, had a lovely view and enjoyed ourselves much."* But later the same summer Sara

Donkey-trap leaving Colwall, c1900.

Child-drivers on the Malvern Hills with their team of donkeys ridden by day-trippers, c1900.

records trying unsuccessfully to return home from Great Malvern by donkey. *"We set off up the hill, in the vain hope of meeting with a donkey but they were all engaged by cheap trippers, who were as thick as blackberries."* (*West Malvern, Valerie Goodbury, 1994*)

The railway line connecting Great Malvern's new station to London had been completed two years before in 1861, bringing three thousand more visitors to the town in the first year, equalling the number of residents. In the same year, complaints from residents

Steam train arriving at Great Malvern Station, 1875.

Great Malvern Station, 1910.

were published in the Malvern Advertiser, reporting that the town was being ruined by the drunkenness and bad manners of these day-trippers, so passengers on day excursions were made to alight at Malvern Link. It's said that this action was taken mainly on the instructions of Lady Foley, who owned much of the land of Malvern. *"These visitors so misbehaved themselves on frequent occasions that the inhabitants petitioned the railway companies against the nuisance. Certain days were then fixed for trips, during which ladies and the more timid residents remained at home."* (*Guide to Worcestershire, John Noake, 1868*)

The town was at its most crowded with excited tourists on 11th July 1861 when 'The Great Blondin', the famous French acrobat and high wire stunt man, was due to perform his tricks *"on the other side of the railway, about half a mile below the hill, near to that old-fashioned house of Pickersleigh"*. A rather shocked old gentleman visitor complained that outside the Foley Arms *"There was a crowd of people, and half were eating pork pies, and half were drinking out of stone bottles. I couldn't believe I was in Malvern. Who'd 'av thought of railways and excursionists to Malvern thirty years ago?"*

Charles Blondin carrying his manager Harry Colcord across Niagra below the falls, in front of the Prince of Wales, Sept 14th 1860.

Blondin owed his celebrity to crossing the gorge below Niagra Falls on a tight-rope whilst blindfolded only two years earlier. Not content with this, on five subsequent occasions he crossed on the high-wire doing different stunts; teetering on stilts, in a sack, trundling a wheelbarrow, cooking and eating an omlette when halfway, and carrying his manager as no-one else would volunteer.

15th century House of Pickersleigh in 1900.

"So magnetic were his attractions, reaching even to the iron districts, that a greater number of people were congregated in Malvern on that day, than had ever been known or heard of in the history of the town. The excursionists had taken the place by storm from an early hour in the morning, and by noon the streets and hill paths were well-nigh impassable." They were *"swarming up the hill's steep sides, some on donkeys and mules, and some on shank's pony"*. At five o'clock those on the hills watching the tight-rope at Pickersleigh through binoculars, could see the *"little acrobat walking and tumbling through the air, over a sea of upturned faces"*. The old gentleman remarked *"I shouldn't have known the place, if it had not been for the hills and the donkeys"*. (*Leisure Hour, Malvern Donkeys, Cuthbert Bede, 1862*)

Many of the wealthier holidaymakers now stayed for the whole

Congested hill paths during "A lively day on the hills".

129

summer season in the newly built station hotels. The impressive 'Imperial Hotel' in Great Malvern, built with Dr Gully's aid, originally boasted water cure, spa and Droitwich brine baths. This hotel, now Malvern St James' School, had its own private access to the station through a corrugated-iron tunnel known as 'The Worm', which still exists in a dilapidated state. The 'Link Hotel' built in the form of a fairytale chateau with ballroom and bar, was later to become a boys' prep school before being demolished in the 1960s.

A steam train emerges from the bridge in front of the Imperial Hotel, 1869.

On 14th November 1876 John Rowberry sailed across the Atlantic from America and the following April came on a day trip to Malvern from Worcester. His letter dated 1st May 1877 makes little mention of the water cure but much of the donkeys. *"We took the train early next morning for Malvern, a place of resort for the pleasure seekers and aristocrats of England, claimed to be a very healthy retreat, in consequence of its altitude. Through the summer season large concourses of people are seen ascending the heights in various ways, on donkeys, in low-wheeled carts or carriages drawn by them, or in baskets carried on either side of them, a complete outfit, according to fancy being readily procured. After refreshing ourselves, we took a stroll up to the heights arriving on the summit about 5 p.m."* (Deseret News, John Rowberry, 1877)

By 1900 up to thirty-five trains a day were bringing regular floods of visitors here, including many day-trippers on excursions from Birmingham and the Black Country. This influx of ordinary tourists continued to cause much annoyance to some of Malvern's more genteel folk, but it was a welcome boost to the donkey-hire trade as the popularity of the water cure itself had been in decline since the 1870s. The hydropath, Dr Wilson had died in 1867 and Dr Gully retired and moved away five years later, after an alleged love affair and being implicated in the scandalous apparent murder of Charles Bravo, the woman's husband. Dr Grindrod died in 1883 and the last remaining practicing hydropath Dr Fergusson was associated with an outbreak of Typhoid fever and went bankrupt in 1913.

Doing the heavy at MALVERN.

Norman May's guide published in 1886 says, *"The Wells are less and less used for medicinal purposes, but are now kept in a condition to satisfy the most fastidious. In fact Malvern is no longer a place where the visitor is shocked and his feelings harrowed by troops of invalids; but is rapidly growing in favour with the robust, healthy and energetic, to whom its hills, golf links and splendid roads afford endless opportunities for recreation and exercise".*

The busy equine road traffic had been added to by two Malvern Brothers, Charles and Walter Santler who firstly made penny-farthing bicycles and then one of the world's first steam driven cars, *"the Dogcart"*, in 1887. Charles, who lived at 'Donnybrook'

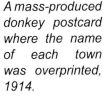

A mass-produced donkey postcard where the name of each town was overprinted, 1914.

Humorous, romantic Malvern postcard, 1914.

on Malvern Common, is said to have frequently ridden a penny-farthing to the top of the Beacon, probably from Wyche Cutting. Then in 1894 they went on to build the *"Malvernia"*, the first four-wheeled petrol driven car in Britain, at the Northumberland Engineering Works in Howsell Road, Malvern Link. This 'horseless carriage' was steered by a tiller and restricted by law to 4mph preceded by a man walking with a red flag, although Charles had secretly driven it at speeds in excess of 20mph. The age of the automobile had now begun. The old 'Malvernia' car was brought out again in the early 20th century and driven in a parade through Malvern by Charles and his friends. Santler cars continued to be produced here until 1922. In 2001 the original car, then owned and restored by Dr Sutton, fetched £146,750 in auction.

In 1897 a Daimler was the first car to be driven to the top of the Beacon, but despite the increasing number of motor vehicles on the roads, several local

Great Malvern Church Street before the automobile.

Horse drawn carriages for hire in Malvern Wells, 1900.

families still operated teams of donkeys until the 1930s. They continued to take goods and people up to the higher springs, top ridges and hill peaks.

Norman May described the wide choice of transport to the top of the Beacon in 1901, including donkeys. *"The splendid paths and drives have now made access to the summit much easier and more practicable than formerly, and the visitor whether strong or less robust will find little difficulty in arriving there, whether on foot or by the aid of the famous Malvern donkeys, or on pony or horse back, or in vehicles. Cyclists and motorists can also reach up to the summit, especially by going to the Wyche and up the new drive, and will even find a notice at the top warning them to go at moderate speed."*

Charles Santler (seated left) and friends drive his first "Malvernia" car in a parade through Malvern, c1920.

The Burden

(Anonymous)

The donkey's heavy burden
made me pause and sigh
as he trod the steep path upwards
but never questioned why,
yet he turned his head and whispered
as he walked slowly by…

"We came from desert fringes
of lands so hot and high,
sun and windstorms scorched us,
our mouths were cracked and dry,
with beaten bodies, skin and bone,
when we lay down to die.

But now I graze on moist hill grass
beneath a soft blue sky
trotting gently homewards
with a twinkle in my eye
and burdens aren't so heavy
with clear streams trickling by."

13 - Donkey Tales

In the 1980s, I found several donkey shoes when digging in the garden of 'The Pillars' at 200 and 202 West Malvern Road, two wooden huts on the corner of Mathon Road that had been village shops. The Pillar family had owned the entire triangle of land from this corner to Croft Bank from 1741 to 1857, known then as *"Pillars Pitch"*. I still have one of the donkey shoes above my summerhouse doorway and these finds made me curious to find out more about the history of donkeys here.

There was a strange old rhyme in West Malvern when I was a child;
> *"Ann Pillar and I fell out*
> *and what was the row about?*
> *Ann has money and I have none*
> *and that was how the row had begun."*

The Pillars seen from Mathon Road with the paddock above. 1980.

The little shops seen from West Malvern Road. 1990.

In 2000 the local Women's Institute published 'The West Malvern Book' with the same poem in it; a fascinating little book drawn from the scrapbook compiled in 1959 by Miss E. Knight. It tells of a Mr Pillar who *"lived in a picturesque thatched cottage at the junction of West Malvern and Mathon Road. His only daughter, who owned St Olave's was considered an heiress. Ann Pillar married Mr Gardiner and left the district."* My mother Mrs Germaine Garrard had bought the huts from a Miss Gardiner in 1955, as her very first antique shops. By that time the bus company, which stopped there, called them *"the Green Sheds"*. Mr Ovens, a shoemaker much respected for his excellent craftsmanship had built them as shops in the 1880s. Each of the two sheds had been occupied separately by various other trades-people over the years and these had included a fishmonger, a chimney sweep, a shoe-mender, and as a wool shop and a 'penny library' or bookshop.

The two occupants until the 1940s were Mr Penfold the shoe-mender, who was revered by St James' School for his repairs because he added each of their girl's initials in studs on the soles so that their boots wouldn't be mislaid, and Mr Burnham the chimney sweep.   He kept a donkey in the paddock opposite to carry his tools and brushes and on some winter nights stabled the donkey beneath one of the shops, which explains the little donkey shoes in the garden.   Before the Second World War Mr Burnham often lent his donkey for village children to ride on outings, sometimes as a Sunday School treat and for the annual village carnival.   In 2008 life-long resident Mrs Marjorie King recalled that once his donkey was taken in the carnival procession from North Malvern carrying a small child dressed as a jockey, but the donkey halted at the Redan Bend and stubbornly refused to go any further, much to everyone's amusement and the child's distress.   Marg, as she is known locally, remembered George Farthing as a child in the 1930s riding this donkey, which he had borrowed to carry his Guy and collect pennies to buy fireworks for use at the annual village bonfire. For many years daily bread was delivered locally by donkey-cart having been made at Summers' Bakery in the village. Mrs Anna

Young donkey-drivers with their child clients on the Beacon path, 1909.

Donkey-cart coming over the hill from Great Malvern and down past the Dingle in West Malvern, c1870.

137

Jackson remembered that before the Second World War, Lisa Birley, the daughter of the vicar at St James' Church, used to hire a donkey for six pence for her to ride carrying eggs over the hill to sell at Great Malvern market. The donkey would then make its own way home again.

I was once told a disturbing old story by another villager, concerning the building of the present St James' Church. Mr McCann built the first church in the village in 1834 and also constructed the Morris Tank and well room at North Malvern in 1836. Only thirty years later the vicar felt the church was too small for the increasing population, so plans were made and funds were raised to build a new one on the northerly corner of adjacent land. A family of 'Tinkers' was evicted from the proposed site and amidst considerable opposition from some villagers the new church began to be built close beside the old one in 1870. One morning the builders arrived to find that the carcass of a dead donkey had been thrown into the newly laid foundations, which some superstitious villagers claimed had put a *"Gypsies curse"* on the new church. Nevertheless the building work was successfully completed and then the old church was pulled down.

The two churches of St James at West Malvern in 1870.

Several of the donkey team owners were matriarchs supporting large impoverished families who lived in small cottages in West Malvern, where the donkeys were often left to graze on the hillsides overnight. *"During the winter season, the Malvern donkeys are turned out upon the hills and waste ground to pick up their livelihood amidst the scenes of their summer labours."* (*Malvern Donkeys, Cuthbert Bede, 1862*)

Girl resting with her hire-donkeys.

Three years after the end of the First World War, in 1921, the enterprising Pitt family came to West Malvern from Wales riding on their fleet of five donkeys, with a white pony to carry the heaviest loads, a journey of four long days. Mrs Kate Pitt led them here and the group included her pregnant daughter Katie, son-in-law Fred George and five-year-old grandson Mick. Mrs Pitt ran their donkey hire business from a pair of modest hill cottages, now called 'The Hermitage' just north of Westminster Bank Springs, and also plied them for hire above St Ann's Well.

For several months after they arrived the children slept in hayricks in one building until parts of the cottages were made habitable. The family then lived on the upper floors, with the donkeys and some pigs housed below in winter to provide warmth. Fred found work at North Malvern quarry and later Mrs Pitt's brother Sam took over the Beacon donkey business until the Second World War and also hired out a donkey cart. In 1991 Kate's 75 year-old grandson Mick George, known locally as a bit of a rogue, recalled his childhood here as a donkey-boy.

"The day used to start for us children at 6.30 a.m. when we would take the donkeys some little distance to collect water from a trough for our household use. We would swing into action with the donkey rides to the top of the Worcestershire Beacon around 11 a.m. when coaches started arriving with visitors from Birmingham and elsewhere in the Midlands. We then worked all day until about tea time." For half-a-crown per person (twelve and a half new pence) they carried passengers in a leisurely fashion on the winding, fifteen minute ride to the top, leaving them to walk down again. *"It may sound as though it was a hard life for the donkeys and for us, but this wasn't the case. The donkeys seemed happy with their lot and certainly lived long lives."* (*Evening News, August 1991*)

Photograph signed by Mick George, taken on his daily journey to the village pub, The Brewers Arms.

Donkey outing by a group of Edwardian women, at the hill crossroads above West Malvern.

Tired donkey boy on the Beacon summit.

Malvern Hills

Dr Luke Booker

Oh! ever could I wander o'er those lawns,
Beside thy streams, thou purest stream that flows!
Climb each bold eminence, and daily find
Some object new of wonder; the deep glades
Traverse, embroidered by intertwining trees;
Drink at the rill that murmurs at my feet
And think it luxury to forever gaze
On the wild scene around me, where conspire
Nature's all-generous offspring to exalt
And warm the soul.

14 - Malvern's Last Donkey-Woman

David Prentice, the renowned Malvern artist, recalls as a tiny child in about 1939, coming to the Malverns by car with his parents where they hired donkeys for the boy and his elderly grandmother to ride up to the Beacon. The donkeys must have belonged to Mrs Alice Betteridge, who was by then the last practicing donkey woman on the hills. Born Alice Davies in 1881, she lived all her life in 'Rock Cottage' at North Malvern, the first cottage on the hill track to the east of the Clock Tower. This cottage was formerly a little tollhouse on the route around North Hill where *"Alice's father would have opened his larger gate for you*

Toll gate at Ivy Scar Rock in about 1880. *Opposite - the same view in 1900.*

Donkey for hire in the Happy Valley, with a donkey shed behind, 1895.

Donkeys making their own way back to their shed, 1895.

144

and your horse in return for a penny".
(Malvern Gazette, Henry Garnett c1947)
Marjorie King remembers that having walked her team and companion pony along the hill path, past Ivy Scar Rock to St Ann's Road, Mrs Betteridge would then tether her donkeys for hire at the hut at the foot of Happy Valley above Great Malvern, where it's said that Bernard Shaw used to enjoy climbing up from the town to spend time talking to her.   Having spent the day ferrying people to St Ann's Well and the top of the Beacon, she returned home with the donkeys each evening, usually watering them a short distance away at the animal trough that used to be beside the now derelict Stocks Fountain in North

Donkeys and drivers climbing St Ann's Road, 1895.

St Ann's Well with hire-donkeys and Blind George Pullen playing the harmonium, 1900.

School girls playing in front of the North Malvern quarries beside the Clock Tower, watched by their teacher, 1901.

Malvern Road. Alice graduated from North Malvern School at fifteen and *"there was within her a deep happiness because all her days could now be spent in the open air, and on the hills she loved so much, and with the animals, sheep and donkeys, for whom she cared."* *(Malvern Gazette, Henry Garnett c. 1947)* From 1896 she worked full-time for her mother Eliza as a donkey-girl on the Beacon, marrying Reginald Betteridge in about 1911. As well as keeping a flock of sheep on Link Common, Mrs Betteridge then had her own pony and a small fleet of donkeys on the North Hill, run with the help of several donkey-boys until the 1940s. She was the third generation of her family to own a donkey-hire business, her grandmother

School girl in a pinafore dress driving donkey riders up Happy Valley, with a donkey shed on right, 1895.

Mary buying the first team of donkeys when the family moved to the tollhouse from Bishop's Frome in Herefordshire in 1854.

In a BBC radio interview broadcast in December 1944, Alice said both her mother Mrs Eliza Davies and grandmother Mrs Mary Bannister had hired out donkeys to take visitors up to the top of the Beacon. *"But a lot of people stopped at St Ann's Well for the healing waters. Doctors used to send people here to take these waters, and the gentry of Malvern let their houses to them for two or three months in the summer. You'd see whole families coming up to the donkey stands in the morning, with baskets all packed for a picnic at the top of the hill. The tiny children who couldn't ride travelled in panniers at the sides of the saddle. They loved it! There were lots of other people running donkeys on the hills too, and there was always a donkey show in the summer in Crown Meadow. Mother and Granny used to take prizes every year."*

The marriage of Reginald and Alice, c1911

Alice Davies (left) with her team of hire-donkeys. The girl on the far right is Winifred Barrows, later headmistress of Lawnside School, Malvern. c1905.

The young Alice soon became expert at describing the beauties of the hills, pointing out landmarks, recounting their histories and taking visitors to favourite spots they loved to see. *"She would lead her donkey to the so-called Gold Mine, the deserted and fruitless tin mines, and she would tell the stories of the British Camp and the legends of Raggedstone, to her own and doubtless the donkey's profit. The Earls of Coventry and Beauchamp became* regular customers *and many more with less high-sounding names."* (Malvern Gazette, Henry Garnett c. 1947)

Jim Rose came to work for Mrs Betteridge as a donkey boy at twelve years old in 1917, earning 2s 6d a week plus food and lodging. His father had a dangerous job as the 'powder-monkey' at the North Malvern quarry and against regulations the boy had walked out of school to get work nearby. Jim looked on Alice as a second mother and worked for her intermittently at the Happy Valley donkey stand until he joined the army, serving for twenty-five years in the Worcestershire Regiment as a blacksmith. *"Tourists on the donkeys were always good for a tip, especially as the boys told them they were 'voluntary' workers. Another 'perk' came to light when a boy called Wadleigh left work one evening, got home and collapsed. The doctor was called post-haste and pronounced the boy 'dead drunk!' Reg Betteridge kept barrels of beer in the donkey sheds..."* (Malvern Between The Wars, Frederick Covins 1981)

But the following years were not kind to Alice when their only child became ill and died in 1914, aged only two and a half, and her husband Reg died in 1924. He had been *"a small farmer, well known as a trainer of horses and recruits in the Worcestershire Yeomanry"*. Jim Rose came back to help but a few years later he joined the armed forces before the outbreak of the Second World War, so Alice then ran the donkey-hire business virtually on her own.

In 1934 Mrs Betteridge spent four or five hours a day standing still with her donkey team while they posed on the hills for the famous artist Dame Laura Knight, who often stayed at the British Camp Hotel or at Sir Barry Jackson's home. In her autobiography 'Magic of a Line' in 1965, Laura Knight recalled with fondness *"carting materials up the wild of a Malvern hillside in late autumn when painting Mrs Betteridge's pony and donkeys."* During 1934 when recovering from a badly broken leg, Laura remembered rather

Sir George Bernard Shaw & Dame Laura Knight in Malvern, 1932.

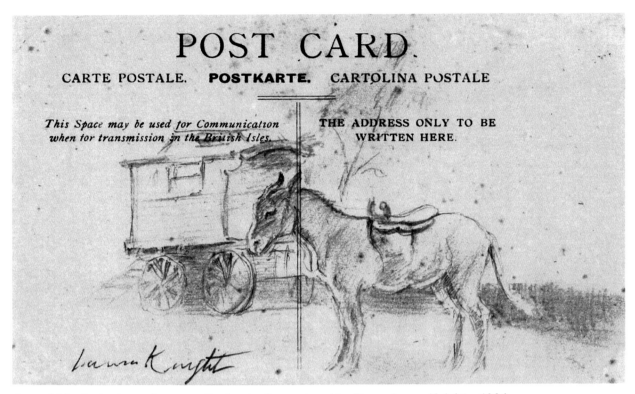

One of Alice's donkeys drawn on the back of a postcard by Dame Laura Knight, c1934.

Blind George Pullen playing his harmonium at St Ann's Well, c1910.

disconsolately climbing the hills with her friend, the poet Conrad Aiken, who tried to cheer her up. *"Once we were sitting on some rough land, half way up to the Worcestershire Beacon, and I asked how he would describe such a scene. 'How would you?' he asked."* Laura then described the landscape below in purely visual terms. *"Conrad said, 'Can't you hear the children playing in that field over there, the old blind man's harmonica at the Well's Tea-rooms, the cars on the road below, the puff-puff of that little train…? And what about the scent of the bracken, the feel of the grassy bank we're sitting on – to say nothing of those people over there who, like ourselves, are resting before climbing to the top?'* I too then opened *my ears and heard Mrs Betteridge urging her old white pony, Kitty, and her donkeys up the hill with their load of youngsters."* She got to know Alice and *"Later that year I spent*

several Autumn months at Malvern, where on the hills every day I made big studies of Mrs Betteridge's Kitty, an old white pony, and her donkeys, which in the summer, took pleasure parties of children to the top." The pony and two donkeys appeared in several of her subsequent paintings.

In 1944 Alice spoke of the decline in the donkey-hire trade. *"I'm afraid the donkeys are dying out now. You see, people began to go abroad for the waters, and then they bought cars and went to the seaside for their holidays, so the families stopped coming here for the summer."*

Alice Davies and her donkey working in Happy Valley, c1900.

Mrs Betteridge's donkeys were now aging and during the war one

Works outing to the seaside, c1920. The first 'Bank Holiday' for workers was created in 1871.

Alice and her donkey-team pose for a photo at the top of Trinity Bank during the war, c1940.

was killed by a fall of rock from the quarry onto its shed. As Alice herself was now approaching sixty, she decided to concentrate instead on improving her flock of hardy Welsh sheep by cross breeding them with Suffolk, Kerry and Clun Forest rams. The two surviving members of her team, a gentle white pony called Tommy and the last donkey, Sally, were now too old to work, but instead of being destroyed they were retired into the care of Mr and Mrs J. Arnold Parish who were keen committee members of the RSPCA. This equine pair of inseparable companions lived out their last years in *"a soft meadow beside an orchard"* in Albert Park Road. The elderly pony Tommy died in

Alice shepherds her flock of sheep grazing on Link Common, c1946.

1952 at the ripe old age of twenty-nine. Mrs Betteridge, Malvern's last donkey-woman, who had by now become well known as *"Malvern's Shepherdess"*, became ill a year later and on January 11th 1955 she died in hospital aged 73.   She was cremated and her ashes scattered by her family on her beloved hills.

But to everyone's surprise the very last hill donkey, Sally, who was by then reaching thirty, lived on for at least another seven years. In January 1962 the Malvern Gazette described her as still *"bright-eyed, indestructible and demure in a dark fur coat, walking a thought gingerly after a pedicure. The vet pronounces her as fit as a flea. Only her sunken back, hollowed by a myriad of burdens, indicates anno domini."*

Sally the last surviving Malvern hire-donkey with Mr Arnold, 1962.

Nicholas Nye
Walter De La Mare

Thistle and darnel and dock grew there,
And a bush, in the corner, of may,
On the orchard wall I used to sprawl
In the blazing heat of the day;
Half asleep and half awake,
While birds went twittering by,
And nobody there my lone to share
But Nicholas Nye.

Nicholas Nye was lean and grey,
Lame of leg and old,
More than a score of donkey's years
He had seen since he was foaled;
He munched the thistles, purple and spiked,
Would sometimes stoop and sigh,
And turn his head, as if he said,
'Poor Nicholas Nye'.

Alone with his shadow he'd drowse in the meadow,
Lazily swinging his tail,
At break of day he used to bray, -
Not much too hearty and hale;
But a wonderful gumption was under his skin,
And a clear calm light in his eye,
And once in a while he'd smile …
Would Nicholas Nye.

Seem to be smiling at me, he would,
From his bush in the corner, of may, -
Bony and ownerless, widowed and worn,
Knobble-kneed, lonely and grey;
And over the grass would seem to pass
'Neath the deep dark blue of the sky,
Something much better than words between me
And Nicholas Nye.

But dusk would come in the apple boughs,
The green of the glow-worm shine,
The birds in the nest would crouch to rest,
And home I'd trudge to mine;
And there, in the moonlight, dark with dew,
Asking not wherefore nor why,
Would brood like a ghost, and still as a post,
Old Nicholas Nye.

BIBLIOGRAPHY

1817 - Chambers' General History of Malvern, Longman, Hurst, Rees, Orme and Brown

1851 - Three Weeks in Wet Sheets, by a Moist Visitor, Hamilton, Adams & Co.

1856 - Illustrated London News, by Cuthbert Bede

1856 - Notes and Queries for Worcestershire, by John Noake, Longman & Co.

1862 - Leisure Hour, Malvern Donkeys, by Cuthbert Bede,

1866 - The Monastery & Cathedral of Worcester, by John Noake, Longman & Co.

1868 - Guide to Worcestershire, by John Noake, Longman & Co.

1872 - British Medical Journal, November 23rd

1876 - Malvern Advertiser, August

1877 - Worcestershire Relics, by John Noake, Longman & Co.

1877 - Malvern Advertiser, March

1886 - Norman May's Guide to Malvern, Norman May & Co. Ltd

1893 - The Horse World of London, by W. J. Gordon

1895 - Malvern Priory Church, by James Nott, John Thompson & Royal Library, Malvern

1901 - The Malvern Country, by Bertram Windle, Methuen & Co.

1904 - Malvern In and Near, by M. T. Stevens & Co

1906 - Ward Lock's Malvern Guide, Ward, Lock & Co. Ltd.

1913 - The Ancient Malvern Priory, by M. C. Stevens Ltd

1914 - Great Malvern Priory Church, by Rev. Anthony C. Deane, Bell & Sons

1921 - Berrow's Journal, January

1924 - Malvern Priory Registers, Lecture by F.C.Morgan

1931 - Malvern Gazette, October

1932 - Worcestershire Book, Federation of Women's Institutes

1943 - Worcestershire in English History, by Alec Macdonald, Press Alliances Ltd.

c1947 - Malvern Gazette, Henry Garnett

1947 - The History of the Worcester Royal Infirmary, by William H. McMenemey

1948 - A Little City set on a Hill, by C.F. Severn Burrow, Priory Press, Malvern

1949 - Worcestershire, by L.T. C. Rolt, Robert Hale Ltd

1953 - Report by C. Judson, MHDC Surveyor and Water Engineer

1962 - Malvern Gazette, January

1964 - A History of Malvern, by Brian S. Smith, Leicester University Press

1965 - The Magic of a Line, by Laura Knight, William Kimber, London

1968 - Malvern Country, by Vincent Waite, J.M. Dent & Sons

1970 - Customs and Folklore of Worcestershire, by Lavender M. Jones, Estragon

1979 - Worcestershire Archaeology & Local History Newsletter

1981 - Malvern Between The Wars, by Frederick Covins, Book Production Services

1991 - Evening News, August, Worcester

1991 - Worcestershire's Hidden Past, by Bill Gwilliam, Halfshire Books

1992 - The Folklore of Hereford & Worcester, by Roy Palmer, Logaston Press

1993 - For The Love of Donkeys, by Dr Elizabeth D. Svendsen MBE, Whittet Books Limited

1993 - Not the Least, the Story of Little Malvern, by Ronald Bryer, Hanley Swan
1994 - West Malvern, by Valerie Goodbury, Valerie Goodbury
2000 - The West Malvern Book, by W.I. and Mrs E. Knight, Capella Archive
2007 - The Forest and Chase of Malvern, by Pamela Hurle, Phillimore & Co.
2007 - Covent Garden Area Trust, by Leana Pooley, Website
2008 - Malvern Memories, Malvern Gazette, by Robert Hale, March

FURTHER INFORMATION

1992 - The Malvern Water Cure, by John Winsor Harcup, Winsor Fox Photos
1992 - The Malverns, by Pamela Hurle, Phillimore & Co.
1994 - Archiving My Own History, by Rose Garrard, Cornerhouse Gallery, Manchester
1994 - Aquae Malvernensis, by Cora Weaver & Bruce Osborne, Cora Weaver
1997 - Donkeys 1992-97, by Donna Burke, Wikipedia
2005 - Images of England; The Malverns, by Brian Iles, Tempus
2006 - Malvern Hill of Fountains, by Rose Garrard, Rose Garrard